INDIA do&don'ts *in* India

By
Priya Sahgal
& Ramalakshmi

Illustrations by
Rashmee Pai

ISBN 978-974-9823-30-9

Copyright 2008 © iGroup Press Co., Ltd.

Published in Thailand by
iGroup Press Co., Ltd.
100 Lang Sanamgolf Krungthep Kreetha Road
Huamark, Bangkapi, Bangkok 10240
Thailand
Tel: +66 2 3223678
Fax: +66 2 7211639
E-mail: info@igrouppress.com

Distributed by
Booknet Co., Ltd.
1173, 1175, 1177, 1179 Srinakharin Road
Suan Luang, Bangkok 10250
Thailand
Tel: +66 2 3223678
Fax: +66 2 7211639
E-mail: booknet@book.co.th

Printed and bound in Thailand by
Amarin Printing & Publishing Public Co., Ltd.

Thank you for buying this book. We welcome your comments.
Please send them to: Email: comments@book.co.th

dos & don'ts in **INDIA**

CONTENTS

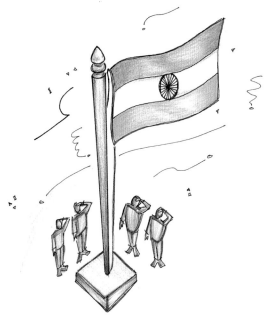

INTRODUCTION

India

India is the *land* of contradiction. You can be sure that anything you say about India, the exact opposite is also true. It is the world's largest democracy and yet tolerates political dynasties; a land where medieval tradition jostles with the label '21st century software-superpower'; the nirvana destination of the world and yet one of worst sanitary systems imaginable; the indigenous tribal people and the jet-setting cosmopolitans; widows are abandoned and worse, yet India's most powerful prime minister was a widow. Everything you have ever heard about India is wrong. And right.

A brief note on a long history

The world's most ancient civilization - the Indus Valley civilization, emerged on the banks of the river Indus five thousand years ago, where the ancient Dravidians lived. Around 2000 BC, new Aryan tribes arrived and settled over much of the subcontinent. This period is significant as it is when much of the Hindu thought and even the Sanskrit language was born. In the 7th century AD the birth, life and teachings of Buddha in the northern Gangetic plain posed one of the most formidable challenges to Hinduism.

Throughout the post Christ era, India was ruled by hundreds of kings with small fiefdoms. Some dynasties such as Cholas, Guptas and Maurya expanded their empire to include almost half of what is now modern India. However, stories of India's riches also attracted Muslim invaders. Thus the medieval period was a long struggle between Hindu kings and Muslim invaders. The Taj Mahal was a by-product of this age.

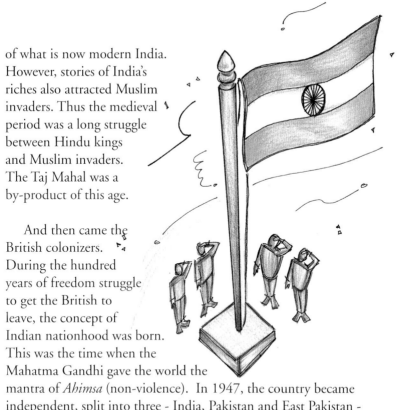

And then came the British colonizers. During the hundred years of freedom struggle to get the British to leave, the concept of Indian nationhood was born. This was the time when the Mahatma Gandhi gave the world the mantra of *Ahimsa* (non-violence). In 1947, the country became independent, split into three - India, Pakistan and East Pakistan - and the seeds of democracy were sown. This was also the time when the first family of contemporary Indian politics, the Nehru-Gandhi family, captured public imagination.

Population

The first thing that hits you about India is its people. The sheer number. A billion people is hard to miss - they brush past you as you walk, they stare at you, they talk to you and the very poorest may ask for money. You are never alone.

Our politicians will have you believe that India is a billion strong. Social activists will tell you that it is so burdened by its numbers, India has to run like an Olympic sprinter just to stay where it is. The politicians will claim that India cannot be ignored as it is a huge market for foreign companies and their products. But the economists will tell you that three hundred million people live in abject poverty and are outside the very notion of 'market'.

No matter how you look at it, India's teeming mass of people is a challenge.

Weather

Indian weather is all about extremes. The north has all four seasons, extreme summer, heavy monsoon, spring and a harsh winter. The south, west and east have no real winter. The best time to visit us is from October to March.

The summer (officially May, June, July, but it begins in April when it's still spring) is scorching and unforgiving. Umbrellas, sun-block creams, hats and white linen... Nothing will help you remain cool. The merciless sun fries your brain and the power cuts cement the torture. But there are ways for the savvy visitor to keep his cool.

DO stay indoors as much as possible. If you must go out, do so before 11 am or after 7 pm.

DO keep a damp hand towel with you always to mop your brow and keep your head cool.

DO drink *lassi* (a mix of curds and water) in the north, buttermilk in the south.

DON'T think you are the only one who is suffering. Even birds fall out of the trees dead. Tires burst in the heat.

DON'T forget modesty even if it's hot. You still have to dress conservatively.

DON'T get caught in the dust storms that sweep the north and the west between April and June. They called *andhi*, a combination of dust and very hot winds. Lasting anywhere up to thirty minutes, it is followed by wonderfully light rain. As soon as the wind picks up strength quickly cover your eyes and run to shelter.

The monsoon lasts from June to September. But Tamil Nadu in the southeast receives most of its rain during the retreating monsoon from October to December. The risk of cyclones along the east coast is greatest between the end of October and early December. The monsoon is a big deal. Farmers, government ministers, presidents and holy men pray for rain every year. Even though we are a software giant and a nuclear power, agriculture remains by a long way, the mainstay of our economy. A good monsoon is not just a good crop. It means headline news, but then so does a bad monsoon.

DO know that the monsoon is a period of joy, and not one to stay indoors. Rain is our deliverance after the sweltering heat of summer. We dance in it, bathe in it, play in it, cycle in it... anything to get wet in the first sweet days of the monsoon.

DO note that the monsoon is the season of love. Romantic poetry is based on this season. To be separated from your lover during the rains, is an unhappy fate. Recall too that the wet look works well with Bollywood songs and dances!

DO carry a rope if you are travelling in the rain. You can tie it across your room to dry your clothes

DO expect to wade through flooded streets in the torrential rains of Mumbai (Bombay) and Kolkata (Calcutta). Traffic comes to a stop, potholes get filled up, offices remain closed, and you may have to walk through brown, muddy waters.

DON'T bring your favourite shoes to India in the monsoon.

DON'T be shy about wearing a polythene bag on your head. Everybody else does.

DO think twice about undertaking long road journeys in the monsoons. It can be hazardous. Landslides are common and buses regularly end up in swollen rivers.

DO expect pollution and low night temperature to contribute to fog in winter mornings in the north. This disrupts train and airline timings a great deal in December and January.

DON'T expect homes and modest hotels to have central heating.

CHARACTER TRAITS

India

There is nothing half-hearted about India. Emotions are heightened, exaggerated and squeezed dry before they are discarded. There are no subtle nuances in the Indian character. We live life king-size. And those of us who try to package Indian-ness into tidy, definite blocks with neat little tags are in for a rude shock: it cannot be done.

So don't hold back when you make friends with an Indian. You may regard him or her as a mere acquaintance but he will treat you with all the warmth and candor of a childhood friend. Just go with the flow and allow yourself to be swept along by the current. It's an exciting ride.

Emotional & warm

There's a distinctively feminine touch here. Remember it's Mother India - she's a woman with all the moods, whimsical willfulness and strength of her gender. This is no harsh fatherland, the people here are warm, nurturing and tolerant.

DO expect heightened emotion, bordering on melodrama. Clearly the maxim here is: emotions are meant to be expressed, not kept bottled up. This is true especially of the north where the heart and lungs dominate. But the warmth is genuine. You're not just a tourist visiting this country. You're a guest in our house. We will embrace you wholeheartedly and do our utmost to make you feel at home.

DON'T be too suspicious if the person you've just met is offering to take you around and is giving you unsolicited advice about your itinerary. Indians love to get involved. Don't be too alarmed if the very first meeting merits an invitation to "come stay with us". The surprise is that it's a genuine invitation. But a word of caution: a tout who wants to fleece you can be just as warm.

DO get physical. One common way to express either intense grief or immense joy is to reach out and physically hug the other person. Words are never enough, at the very least the news will merit a slap on the back. But a word of caution: the hugging is usually restricted to the same gender.

DO notice the colours. Indians express emotion through colour. Our clothes are gay and vibrant. Even men don't hesitate to wear pink and yellow coloured shirts. And if he is a Sikh (a bearded man from Punjab) wearing a turban, the chances are it'll be a bright colour that often coordinates with the colour of his shirt. And matches his socks.

DON'T expect subtlety. Indians speak loud and rarely whisper. When they weep, they wail. When they laugh, they fall all over. If you laugh at their joke once, be ready to hear ten more.

Patience

Indians are very patient. It's an acquired habit. Nothing moves on time, so the key to survival really depends on how you play the waiting game. And we have mastered the art of killing time. Conversation meanders. Directions are never to the point. Our walk is languid and slow rather than brisk (except when we whiz around parks for our morning constitutional). We are rarely on time, hence the joke that IST really stands for Indian Stretchable Time.

DO say *"Koi Baat Nahin"* ("it doesn't matter") if someone steps on your toes, or keeps you waiting for hours. Losing your temper won't help. Being stoic will. Even if your toe is really hurting. It's alright.

DO believe in tomorrow. India doesn't just believe in the maxim that what you don't do today can easily be done tomorrow. It invented it. Don't fight it. It's a losing battle. Just accept the fact that tomorrow is another day.

DO be wary of the omnipresent, *"chalta hai"*, which means "anything goes". Don't be taken in by the seemingly easy-going attitude to life. This is merely an excuse for incompetence, delay and laziness.

DON'T rush an Indian: everything in our country takes time. The sign may say Fast Food, but it'll still take half an hour to deliver your meal. The shopkeeper will shuffle around, make conversation with you before he finally hands over your goods. It's no use being impatient. You'll only antagonize and things will move even slower.

Curious

You've barely said hello and you've been asked your entire life history. If you're alone, you'll be asked why. If you're with a companion, you'll have to explain the exact nature of the relationship. When we ask about your job, be warned that the next question will be about your salary, in exact figures and the right currency. Well, it beats talking about the weather!

DO realize that asking too many questions is not considered bad manners. Indians are curious and talkative. When they want to know your life story, they are not being intrusive, just friendly. Ask us one question and we'll ask you ten questions questioning why you asked that question before coming up with the answer!

DO accept that if there is an accident or an altercation on the road, it'll cause a jam as every passer-by and passing car will stop and get involved in the argument. Everybody has an opinion but few will offer help. If you have the time, join the crowd and voice an opinion. Even if you did not see the accident happen, nobody will question your right to do so.

DON'T be offended by the 'great Indian stare'. You will be stared at wherever you go. Even by the person sitting right next to you. We don't think it is offensive. If we find you interesting enough we'll even point you out to our children so they can stare too.

Religious

We are very religious. There's a Hindu temple on every street corner. Holy men are revered in every aspect of life: religious, social and political. Even if the Indian does not believe in God, he will not scoff at God. After all, *dadiji's* (grandma) bedtime stories about UFO-like men descending on earth with extraordinary powers can't all be wrong.

The average Indian Hindu believes in *karma*, fate, God and reincarnation. The most common succor in times of hardship is: It is my destiny. Nothing could have been done to avoid it. And for every mishap the reaction is, God is great, it could have been worse. Touch wood.

DON'T be surprised, but what upholds the law and morality in our country is not the sleepy *thanedar* (constable), it's the belief in rebirth: that if you do good now, you can change your destiny in the next life. It's confusing. But who said India was not confusing?

DO feed milk to a statue. And pretend it's drinking it. Such is the power of religious belief that once an entire nation fed milk in a teaspoon to a stone statue of Lord Ganesh, our much beloved elephant headed deity. The story was that somebody's Ganesh statue was drinking milk and everyone wanted a part of the miracle. Don't argue. This is India. It's a miracle.

Diverse

You've read the words multicultural, diverse and multi-faceted. Great. Because now you'll finally learn what these mean.

A quick rule of thumb:

The East: Soft-spoken, artistic, pretentious and clannish.

The North: Boisterous, ostentatious but generous and very emotional.

The South: Intelligent, simple-living and emotionally restrained.

The West: Cool, stoic and seriously business-minded.

DON'T treat this as the bible, just an illustration of some distinctive regional character traits:

There was a very poor Bengali (eastern India) farmer with a gravely ill child. The father rushed to the doctor, but as he had no money, the doctor refused to attend to the child. The child died, the Bengali wept and composed a moving elegy on his dead child.

Same scenario, but this time it is a farmer based in U.P. (north India). The father went to the doctor and pleaded but to no avail. He then went to his local politician, who was not home. The child died. But when the politician returned he gave a call to his party-workers and they held a *rasta roko* (stopping the traffic) for eight hours as a protest.

Next scenario. This time it was a Sikh child (from Punjab, west India) who was gravely ill. Its father pleaded and wept but when the doctor persisted in his refusal to attend to the child, the Sikh took out his *kirpan* (sword) and threatened to kill the doctor. The doctor promptly attended the child. The child recovered.

Same scenario with the South Indian, who will pull out a rule book of medical ethics and laws and give the doctor a lecture. The sick child will just have to wait.

Proud

DON'T criticize India: Indians are the most forgiving people in the world except when they feel you're running down their country. It's akin to insulting their mother. At the same time, don't be too surprised to hear them complaining about India. That's their prerogative - not yours.

DO compliment Indians on their ancient heritage: They are very aware of their rich cultural past. All the tourist blurb will point out that it was India which gave the world the Zero and the Decimal and was the site of one of the oldest civilizations of the world. We also consider ourselves as morally, intellectually and spiritually superior to the West which is regarded as materialistic and morally-bankrupt. (Despite this, heaven and earth will be moved for a green card.)

DON'T talk down to Indians. We believe we are just as good as you and expect to be treated as an equal. Do not be condescending. Third world jokes do not work.

DON'T make comments about skin colour. Indians are the most colour conscious people in the world. A 'fair' bride is what matrimonial ads are about (more about this later.) In case you didn't get the message, there is even a popular face cream called: Fair & Lovely. White is good. Black is bad.

Disorganised

DO be rowdy: Indians do not know how to form a queue. There will always be a mass of people, pushing, struggling, throwing their arms and legs at various angles in front of a counter. Not one will stand in an orderly line so you shouldn't try to either. The only way to get things done is to join in and jostle. It's an art. Lean your bodyweight counter-wards, push the person in front of you and flail your arms vigorously to clear your way and keep shouting at the top of your voice: "Don't push me"!

DON'T expect 'them' to follow rules: it's not a character flaw. It's a way of life. Even if you pay your bills on time, you'll still have to make three trips to the electricity office on account of some billing error. It's easier to grease the billing clerk's palm on the first trip and save yourself the next two rounds.

DO learn the catchwords. The first thing the clerk tells you is "It is not possible." Don't get alarmed. This is a sign to begin bargaining for the bribe amount. The system of corruption is so well regulated that there is an established formula to be recited when handing over the bribe : "a little something for your kids". No matter that the bribe taker is a bachelor.

DON'T be irritated by the constant fidgeting. As a case study watch the crowd near an elevator. Nine out of ten will push both the Up and Down buttons regardless of the direction they are headed. It's just that they need something to do while waiting for the elevator.

DON'T be disgusted by the display of private acts in public. Indian men scratch their private parts in public. 'Mining' the nose while we're thinking very hard is an innocent pastime. We're concentrating so hard as to render us quite oblivious to your shocked stare.

Moralistic

There is a conspiracy of silence as far as sex and morals are concerned. It's not uncommon for even the village feudal lord to have a 'secret' mistress. The middle class expects and grudgingly accepts extra-marital affairs. But no one flaunts it.

DON'T talk sex. Just do it quietly if you must. Sex is not an accepted topic of conversation. Not in sophisticated drawing rooms or under the village tree. It is however, the subject of whispered gossip. Never mind if you've just seen a Hindi-movie replete with scantily clad women, lewd comments, and explicit 'eve teasing'. That's tabloid. Real life is supposed to be more restrained. So don't try to break the ice with the village belle by winking at her. It may work for the celluloid hero. But it's a definite no-no for you.

Did you come to bay-watch? Then you're in for a disappointment. Most women, except for the nubile metro girls frequenting the tourist beaches in Goa, rarely wear a skimpy bathing suit. And almost never a bikini. They simply wade into the water, six yards of sari and all. For them, the sea is not a place for energetic breast strokes. That's for the men, and pardon the pun! The modest woman (and that's almost all of us) just takes a coy dip. Or offers a silent prayer.

LANGUAGES

India

India, contrary to what the patriotic brochures declare, does not speak in one language. The constitution recognizes 18 of them, most of which are regional. The National Academy of Letters has added four more to reach a count of 22 literary languages. But this is not all. Every ten kilometers the dialect changes. People are passionate about language. It is the currency of culture in India.

DON'T speak Sanskrit on the street. Like Latin, the Indian languages derive their soul from Sanskrit. Again, like Latin, it is no longer used in everyday conversation, but almost all Indian languages contain Sanskrit words. While it is the mother-language, it is also a dead language. The only people to use it are Hindu priests who learn the language for the Sanskrit chants.

DO praise the rich heritage of Sanskrit if you meet an upper caste Indian. **DON'T**, if you are with a lower-caste Hindu. Remember, Sanskrit is how the Brahmins kept the 'untouchables' out. It was the language of the priests and the learned. (More about this in 'Caste and Class' chapter).

DO remember that language has always been stuff of politics in India. When the constitution was being written after independence, India almost tripped over its multilingual tongue and fell apart.

DON'T speak Hindi in the south. Hindi, a northern language is resented by the South Indians. Back in the 1950s, they did not want it as the official language. Instead, they preferred English, the language of the departed colonizers to Hindi. "Hindi never, English ever", was the slogan as they immolated themselves on the streets. If you are in the south, you can get around with English. In fact if you speak in Hindi, many southerners will reply in English. It's a bit like speaking English to a Frenchman.

DO be aware, if you are dealing with bureaucrats, clerks and officers in the government departments, then you can get by with your English. If you are in a police station to file a complaint, you can write it in English. They will translate it into a regional language.

DON'T be surprised if your attempts at Hindi meet with blank looks. Even Hindi has its own tinge of politics in today's India. There is the Hindi which is formal, stilted and has a heavy dose of Sanskrit. This is used in formal communications, or by Hindu nationalists who want to prove a political point about their Hindu roots. And in your Hindi help books. Then there is Hindustani. It is informal and has a large dose of Urdu. Hindustani represents the confluence of Hindus and Muslims.

DO remember to add the suffix *'ji'*. Even if you don't know Hindi, just add the *ji* to anybody's name or designation. It's a gesture of respect to the person referred to. They will think you are being respectful and the meeting would warm up immediately.

DO note that culture changes with language in India. The states were organized largely along lines of language. But Punjabi and Tamil are not just different languages, the people who speak them follow different cultural lifestyles and rituals. People who speak Punjabi have a different set of festivals and customs from the neighbouring Hindi-speaking Uttar Pradesh.

DO speak with your hands. If you are in a place where nobody speaks English, then just use your hands and gesticulate a lot even as you continue speaking in English. We'll figure you out. Like Italians, Indians use gestures before they even begin to use words. Don't worry, even if they do not speak English, many Indians end up using a lot of English words unknowingly. And unlike the Thais or other Southeast Asians, we'll persevere with you and not just walk away mumbling "crazy foreigner".

DON'T get confused by the way Indians shake and nod their heads. While they shake their heads to say No, they don't always nod to say Yes. Instead, they oscillate. It also means Okay.

English

The country's educated elite reads English. Although the Indian novel in English is on the ascendant internationally, there is always an argument that English does not represent the soul of India. The Indian subcontinent has been speaking English for 300 years now. Or at least, some version of the Queen's English.

There are those in the cities who speak, read and write in English with a lot of ease. Then there are those in the smaller cities for whom English is a ticket up the social ladder.

DON'T speak in English if you go to villages in the north, you will rarely find people who understand it with the exception of the school teacher. In the southern villages, more will be eager to climb on to the English ladder.

It is ironic, but in the absence of one dominant Indian language weaving the nation together, English serves as a bridge across the multitude of India's languages and cultures.

Hinglish

But in the 1990s, with the rise of the middle class, a new language took over: Hinglish. Cable TV promoted this 'language' whose essence is Hindi with a liberal sprinkling of English words thrown in to the mix. Another example would be beginning your sentence in Hindi and finishing it in English. Even the news is read out in Hinglish because we don't have readily understood words for computer jargon and many new technologies. Hinglish is a defiant new language.

It defied the officious English and Hindi. It speaks to the class that thinks in Hindi but speaks English. A class that watches HBO movies at home night after night, but rushes home to watch Bollywood releases every Friday. A class that likes to have a pizza delivered but is more at home with butter chicken. It's about new aspirations without totally disentangling yourself from your roots.

The first politician who spoke this language was late Prime Minister Rajiv Gandhi, and he was ridiculed. But then that was the eighties. That was before cable TV.

DON'T miss the irony. India fought hard to get rid of the British, but showed no desire to get rid of their language. We've adopted it, changed and twisted it. Made it our own.

DO believe us when we say that India makes a lot of money because of its comfort in English. India is a software superpower because of English. It will soon be the call centre capital of the world because of English. That person you're reporting your lost credit card to is in Mumbai, not Minneapolis. English is our strategic edge. Now, if only Filipinos spoke Chinese...

DO listen carefully to our English accent. It helps you to pin down a person socially. You can also make out if he has gone to a cheap, government-run school or a fancy convent or private school. It will also help you identify whether he is from the south, east, west or the north.

DON'T be surprised to discover that some English words are exported Indian words. Sepoys, charpoys and catamaran became part of the English language during the colonial rule. Yoga, guru, nirvana, mantra and karma were popularised when The Beatles came to India to romance Hinduism. Curry, kebabs and tandoori came with the burgeoning Indian community living in England. And we mustn't forget what all of Indian and Britain stops for: chai. That's tea to you Americans.

Other examples of words with Indian origins are jodhpurs (riding breeches), khaki, pundit, pariah (lower caste Hindus in Tamil Nadu), thugs, veranda, dekko, dacoit, mulligatawny (soup), kismet, and bungalow.

DO enjoy the spiced-up version of English in India. Indians will speak in English and yet to you, it may sound like an alien language. Whatever you do, don't tell him or her to speak English when that is what they're doing.

There is an entire body of English usage, phrases and words that only Indians seem to understand. Indian English could perhaps best be defined as a language written or spoken by Indians in the belief that it is English.

- The most common is the use of the present continuous verb. "I am not knowing this person," or "I am wanting to go to a movie", or "I am not having time to meet you."

- If you go to small cities and towns, the hotels that serve liquor put up a sign outside saying, 'permit room available.' It just means they have the permit to serve liquor and a room is available for that.

- Or, outside restaurants and shops, there are signs that will say 'today cash, tomorrow credit'. It just means you pay cash. Now.

- Or on the back of highway trucks, signs will say, 'OK TATA, Horn Please'. This means you are encouraged to blow your horn. Tata is just the name of the company. You are not being wished goodbye.

- The other more famous sign to be seen on the back of trucks is, 'Use dipper at night', which means dip your headlights when a vehicle is approaching. (Please note: it is not an advertisement for a condom)

- Outside restaurants in small towns you'll often find, 'Meals Ready'. It means fast service.

- All over the place on menus, in hotel lobbies, in taxis and cinemas you'll be welcomed by 'wel-come', sort of 'Well, come here. We're pleased to see you.'

- Sign outside Xerox shop: 'Xerox done in all languages.' Doesn't mean anything.

- A common sign outside fabric shops is 'Suiting, Shirting and Panting'. It means fabric available to make suits, shirts and pants, not 'We're short of breath in our rush to serve you'.

- Other Indian words that either don't exist elsewhere or have been carried by Indians to their new country of work: 'pre-pone' (as opposed to post-pone, for example, move your meeting forward); 'non-vegetarian' (since there are so many vegetarians, this becomes an identity in itself); 'non-veg jokes' (dirty jokes); 'eggetarians' (you are a vegetarian who thinks eggs are okay); 'lakh' (one hundred thousand); 'foreign-returned' (you are one of those privileged Indians who has travelled or lived abroad but returned to live in the Motherland); 'slowly-slowly' (just over-emphasis, in case slowly doesn't do the trick); 'long-long road', 'little-little'; 'eve-teasing' (sexual harassment of ladies); 'B.A. failed' (you sat the exam and failed).

Unique Indian usage can be fun and succinct: 'we're like this only' (you can't change us, or, take it or lump it); 'please do the needful' (bureaucratic language that means I am not going to give you specific instructions but you are expected to understand what is part of your duty); 'yours brotherly' (your brother); ' number two' (as opposed to all things legal and above-board).

It's not all nouveau English. While reading some newspapers you can be forgiven for thinking you're not in the 19th century. Outdated words and phrases still used today include; 'pachyderms' instead of elephants; 'scribes' for journalists; 'thespians' for actors (not a misprint for lesbians); 'bad elements' and 'anti-social elements' for gangsters and hooligans; 'fissiparous' and 'bifurcate' for split in two: "turn right when the road bifurcates"); 'our simian friends' of course, means monkeys, not friends who look like monkeys!

POLITICS AND ROYALTY

Politics

DO note that India is the world's largest democracy. We remind the world of this at every opportunity especially because China and Pakistan aren't! This also explains the chaos and cacophony. Apart from the two main political parties, there are over 48 regional parties that have recently appeared in the national arena. Often, the governing coalition is a combination of as many as 23 small parties. All this makes the Indian parliament a very colourful panorama to watch.

DON'T confuse the Gandhis. There's Mahatama Gandhi and then there's the Gandhi family, the surname of India's leading political dynasty. Neither is related.

DO note that the Indian politician is usually a political caricature in a white kurta-pyjama (long shirt and trousers). He is depicted as the epitome of corruption and sloth and often has a criminal record. India has little respect for its politicians, yet this breed of venal men and women continue to call the shots.

DON'T be misled by the contempt. The Indian politician is a very important figure in a country where influence peddling, name-dropping and bribes are often the only way to get your work done.

DO realize that it is the two main national parties that hold the key to India's polity. The Congress is India's oldest political party and follows a socialist, secular ideology. It is run by the Gandhi dynasty. In fact, the dominant ideology of the Congress family can easily be mistaken as blind allegiance to the Gandhi family. This also explains why the Italian born Sonia Gandhi was asked to lead the Congress, because she had married into the right family.

DON'T miss the wave of saffron, the colour of the other dominant group, the Bharatiya Janata Party. The BJP is often described by the western media as the 'right wing Hindu nationalist party'. Self-appointed custodians of Hinduism, the party came to power using religion as its calling card. You've heard of the rabid, fundamental political animal? That's the BJP at its worst. There are, however, some moderates at the helm of the party to give it the required veil of acceptability. That's just a game to stay in power. And it failed.

DO note that communism may have been defeated the world over but not at the Communist Party headquarters in India. The Left parties in India have only one role to play on the national arena: that of opposition. At the state level, the Left have for decades been in power in West Bengal and are marginal but influential players in Kerala. When the Left joins a ruling coalition, it soon establishes itself as the voice of dissent. Communism has no place in India at a time of liberalisation and free market economy. But someone still has to break this news gently to these successors of Marx and Lenin.

DON'T be shocked but corruption is not much of an issue in India. One former prime minister has been charged and one chief minister spends half her time ruling Tamil Nadu and the other half in courts fighting allegations of corruption. Most legislative members from the Hindu heartland of U.P. and Bihar have been arrested at some point or the other.

DO recall that India was British so we follow the Westminster system of governance. The lower house or the Lok Sabha consists of 545 elected representatives. The ruling party has to have a majority here. The Upper House, or the Rajya Sabha, is the House of Elders. Or that is how it was meant to be. In recent times, the moneyed lot has taken over, with industrialists and lobbyists seeking this as a route to the corridors of power. And as a result, there is more black hair than grey to be found there. And black money too undeclared to the taxman.

DON'T miss out on the circus of elections. It is the biggest festival in India. In a perfect world, it comes every five years. But there is something called 'too-much-democracy' that thrusts this festival upon the people more frequently than they bargain for.

DON'T just look at elections as a huge expenditure for the nation. This is probably the only time the poorest of the poor are wooed big time by the ruling class. With money, dreams, promises and some alcohol.

Royalty

When you look at the noisy and bustling Indian democracy, you may wonder whatever happened to the land of Maharajas, especially if you're British. Well they live, some in politics, others in palace-turned-heritage hotels and others losing on the polo grounds.

DO your best to address them by their titles such as Maharaja or Raja saheb. They expect it and like it. In their erstwhile kingdoms, they are still revered by villagers, even though the largesse has stopped flowing. Many of their former subjects believe that life was better under royalty than under democracy.

DON'T forget that this is one of the reasons the royalty flirts with democratic politics. As elected lawmakers they retain their power in the new era, even if it means they have to occasionally jump into the dirt and grime of election campaigning.

DON'T think they are all rich millionaires. Many are paupers, just holding on to their crumbling palaces, *havelis* (mansions) and egos. Others though are fabulously wealthy with property and business in and outside India. Not to mention jewels, antiques, art and vintage cars.

DON'T expect them not to flaunt their status and title at family marriages and funerals. These are often a grand display of power, remaining wealth and lineage. And their private escapades, be it on the polo fields or a secret elopement, still make big news in the society pages.

DO look for cities that have palace-hotels, especially in Rajasthan, India's western desert state. They tend to be expensive, but they come with a heavy dose of history, Raj nostalgia and sometimes even a brief brush with the remnants of the royal family. The last public symbol of royalty was when India's international airline, Air India, had a stout, genial and bowing Maharajah as its airplane icon. But new India would have none of it, and removed him in favour of the horse-riding archer in the early 1990s.

RELIGION

India

Daily life in India is charged with religious activities. Religion permeates both family and personal life and Indians are some of the most religious people in the world. It is very difficult to separate Indian cultural life and rituals from Hinduism unless you are Muslim.

India is an officially secular but predominantly Hindu nation. But be warned, secularism here doesn't mean there is no religion in the state policies and activities. It just means all religions have equal status. Out of one billion people, more than eighty percent are Hindus and 14 percent are Muslims, the second largest in the world. Christians, Sikhs, Buddhists, Jains and Parsis are the other minorities.

Hinduism

Hinduism is not a revealed religion. This means it has no founder and has no definite teachings.

DO know that there is no central Hindu organization like the church, no universally recognized leaders, and no definite set of scriptures. It evolved out of a cluster of loosely interwoven system of traditions, rituals and cults.

DON'T be confused by Hinduism's many gods and goddesses. It's okay if you just remember the main ones: Lord Shiva, Vishnu, Brahma, Lakshmi, Ganesh and Durga.

In fact the very word Hinduism refers to a geographical entity - it is derived from the word *Sindhu*, the Sanskrit name for the Indus River. The term Hinduism was not given by Hindus. It was the early European who gave this name to the body of religious practice.

The religion was born out of the contact between the indigenous people of the Indus River Valley region and the Aryan invaders who came in the second millennium BC. The *Vedas* and the *Upanishads*, the body of ancient Sanskrit literature, were brought by the Aryans. The *Vedas*, composed between 1200 and 600 B.C. have been handed down by ancient sages and holy men. Although the *Vedas* are regarded as the purest and the most sacred of Hindu thought, almost no modern Hindu follows and practices them anymore.

Basic beliefs

Dharma is one of the basic tenets. It means duty, law, ethics, virtue and custom. It denotes social behaviour and a set of obligations.

Karma is the belief that every action and deed has an effect. It determines the nature of your next birth, the length of your next life and the experiences of that life. This is central to achieving liberation in Hindu thought.

Rebirth is the belief that the soul is caught in a never ending cycle of rebirths where upon death, the soul enters another body. Whether the next birth is a human or an animal is determined by the *karma* of the previous life. Only when there is a life free of sin will the soul be finally set free from the wheel of life and death and attain *moksha* or nirvana, salvation.

Sacred rivers

DO revere our rivers. When you look at the state of Indian rivers, you may wonder why. But rivers are holy for Hindus. A number of pilgrimages are undertaken to riverside temples. In fact in Hindu thought, not just rivers but trees and animals are also worshipped. This comes from the animistic origins of Hinduism where nature worship was central.

The Ganga or Ganges is the holiest of Hindu rivers. Along its banks are dotted the holy pilgrimage sites of Varanasi (Banares), Haridwar and Rishikesh. The Yamuna river (you will see this flowing in New Delhi and behind the Taj Mahal in Agra) is the mythical Saraswati river.

Dial-a-God

DO know that there is a God for everything. For money there is the Goddess of Wealth, Lakshmi. For knowledge, there is Saraswati. For good luck there is always the omnipresent, rotund, elephant-headed God Ganesh. For power and strength, there is the Goddess Kali or Durga. For fearlessness, there is the monkey God Hanuman.

The Threesome, the trinity, the trio

DO remember that there is Brahma, the Creator of the Universe. There are almost no temples for this four-headed God. Vishnu is the Preserver. Vishnu, reclining on a multi-headed serpent, has several forms, including the playful Krishna, the dutiful Rama. Then there's Shiva, the Destroyer of evil. He has a crescent moon and a river locked in his hair. He keeps his third eye (on the forehead) closed. It is said if he opens it, the universe will burn to ashes. In our religious stories he is quite a hit with the ladies and is known to enjoy marijuana.

Story time

The great Hindu epics are *Ramayana* and *Mahabharata*. Like all good stories, these also take thousands of verses and hundreds of complex characters and situations to tell you that Good always wins over Evil.

Ramayana is the story of Rama and forms the foundation of much of the moral tradition of Hinduism. It is the common man's Bible. Rama is the epitome of the ideal King and ideal man.

Mahabharata is the story of two sets of descendants fighting for a kingdom. The best known portion of this epic is the *Bhagavad-Gita* (song of the blessed one) which teaches the virtues of detached *karma* and duty.

Spiritual tourism

DO calm your restless soul by taking a dip in India's spiritual cauldron. You can visit Varanasi and bathe in the holy Ganga to liberate your soul from the cycle of endless rebirths. After this, please do go back to your hotel and have a clean shower. To see Lord Buddha's Tree of Enlightenment go to Gaya and listen to the sonorous chanting of monks. This is meant to put you off *maya*, the world of illusion. For a bit of Goddess worship, try the arduous trek up the wish-fulfilling Vaishnav Devi hill-temple in Jammu. Legend has it that only the purest of hearts can squeeze through the narrow cave opening to reach the *sanctum sanctorum*. There is a lot of singing and dancing involved in the trek.

At the temple

DO dress modestly when you visit a temple or any place of worship including churches and mosques. Although there are no rules, revealing tight clothes should be avoided. Clothes that cover rather than reveal are the rule.

DO remember that although you can take a photo in most temples, you cannot take pictures of the idol or the main deity or anywhere near the *sanctum sanctorum*.

DON'T expect to be admitted to all temples. Some are just for Hindus. Even if you're a follower of the Hare Krishna cult and you bang your drum and tinkle your finger bells, you may still be refused entry. Hinduism is acquired by birth, not choice.

DON'T wear your shoes/slippers inside a temple. In some temples you may even be asked to wash your feet. In others you will be asked to remove all forms of leather including wallets, belts and watchstraps.

DON'T touch the priest at the temple. He may not like that. Some priests are more liberal but always wait to see if he shakes hands with you first.

DON'T enter if you are having your monthly period. To do so is considered a defilement of the temple.

DO be aware that there are temples for just about everything including transvestites and eunuchs, prostitutes too. And if you don't like rats, avoid those that encourage these squeaking, scurrying but revered rodents.

DO know that beggars congregate outside Hindu temples. Hindus believe it is good *karma* to give alms - money, food - outside temples. If you want to join in, you may want to carry loose coins with you when you visit a temple. You might prefer to give food, bananas and apples for example. But believe us, those outstretched hands want to be crossed with silver, not snacks!

DO take part in the *puja*, the ritual of worship. This could be a mere *darshan*, which means just peeping in to take a look at the idol and standing for a couple of minutes with eyes closed and hands folded. Or it could be a more elaborate ritual where you bring in fruits, flowers, coconut, camphor and fragrant incense sticks on a plate and chant a few Sanskrit hymns or have the tem-ple priest chant them for you. Either way it is an individualized way of worship. Although there are times when singing and praying is done in groups, most of the time it is a personal worship.

DO choose your day. Hindu Gods and Goddesses have a favourite day that is also auspicious for devotees. If

Hanuman, the monkey God, is your favourite, for best results pray on Tuesday. You could also choose an indirect way by feeding bananas to 'our simian friends'. That would please him too although if you are in Delhi you might get disapproving looks or even get arrested because monkeys have become marauding packs of chattering hooligans in the city. Mondays are Shiva's favourite.

DO circle the temple's inner area if you are in the south. South Indians believe in a circumambulation of the *sanctum sanctorum* building at least three times. Some people engage in all kinds of complicated ways of doing the rounds as part of their penance. They also prostrate on the floor in front of the idol at the end of the ritual. The north Indians do it more subtly. They just touch the threshold with their hand and bring the fingers to their forehead. Same idea, one involves more exercise that's all.

DON'T hesitate to watch the Gods bathe in the South. In south Indian temples, the priest bathes the idol at least twice a day with water, milk, honey and sandalwood paste. And you get to watch it. Notice worshippers go into religious ecstasy or stand in rapt attention and devotion during the bath. As a result, south Indian temples use more water and the floor is inevitably wet. So **DO** be cautious as you meet and greet the Gods and Goddesses.

DON'T conclude that the idol is the be-all and the end-all of Hindu thought. You are supposed to transcend the idol and finally be one with the invisible. Hinduism is replete with such seeming contradictions. Atheism is also part of Hindu thought. To say "There is No God" is also part of devotion in Hinduism. Because one of the philosophies is that God is inside you, that you are God. Good for the ego, isn't it?

DO understand that there is no place for confession in Hinduism. If you have sinned you have to bear the consequences. That is *karma*. If it seems too harsh for you, don't worry, the consequence will come only in your next birth. So you are okay in this lifetime.

DO remember that you cannot become a Hindu. If you have aspirations in that direction, the most you can do is chant *Hare Krishna* like The Beatles.

DON'T think temple priests are holy men of great wisdom. They are merely men who have learnt to perform temple rituals in Sanskrit. If you have a deep, philosophical question about life and death, then you may want to seek out *swamis* and *gurus* in ashrams.

DON'T be fooled into thinking every *sadhu* in dreadlocks and saffron robes is a holy man. Many of them are men who have left their homes and families and wander about smoking hashish because Lord Shiva was known to imbibe now and again. If you are looking for a guru, be very choosy. Don't just pick up anybody on the street or temple corner.

DO avert your eyes and scurry away, ladies, when you come across a naked *sadhu*, more often that not smothered in ash and thus looking like a ghost. They can be saucy and cheeky. Some of the *sadhu* 'tribes' eschew clothing. Nude *sadhus* tend to congregate at Shiva temples at *Shiva ratri*, a major festival; and at *Khumb Melas*, huge gatherings of the pious come together for mass worship.

Islam

Islam came to India in the eleventh century with the early Arab and Turkish invaders. A succession of dynasties culminated in the grand period of Mughal rule in the sixteenth century. Muslims constitute India's largest religious minority, about 14 percent.

DO be aware that under the Mughals, Indian art and literature flourished and India produced some of its best architecture and calligraphy. In Indian classical music, the genre of *thumri* was born in the Mughal courts; *kathak* in Indian classical dance; and mughal miniature paintings.

DON'T forget either that the conquering Muslims also brought with them their distinctive cuisine of sweet and sour flavours and spices and the combination of fruit and meat in perfectly balanced dishes.

DON'T also forget the Taj Mahal was built by the Mughals. Some of the finest examples of architecture came from the confluence of Hindu and Islamic features. A variety of domed structures and tomb complexes incorporated Hindu architectural elements too. Fatehpur Sikri, near Delhi, is a supreme example of Mughal architecture and intricate detail.

DO note that the Urdu language, both mellifluous and very poetic and still spoken in north India and of course Pakistan, was born out of the mingling of Hindus and Muslims, native Indian languages and Persian.

DON'T think that the spread of Islam across India was achieved by forcible conversion. Islam succeeded through patronage by the new rulers of Muslim saints and teachers. Hindus also adopted Islam for their own reasons, perhaps to escape untouchability that has no place in the teachings of Islam. And some Muslim leaders, especially Emperor Akbar, found pleasure in Hindu philosophies, culture and other teachings.

DO know that at the time India gained her independence from the British, a separate country, Pakistan, was created for a large section of Muslims living in India's north, east and the west. Millions of Muslims migrated to the new homeland while millions more remained in India asserting their faith in India's secular ideals. East Pakistan eventually became Bangladesh. The carving up of colonial India into India and Pakistan caused bloodshed.

DON'T think that Indians have forgotten the trauma of partition. It comes up every time Hindus and Muslims, or India and Pakistan fall out with each other.

Sikhism

Sikhs are one of the most recognizable Indians around the world. Beards and turbans give them a distinctive profile. They comprise about two percent of India's population. Yet because they are a conspicuously successful and hard working people, their numbers seem much more than they really are. Sikhs are from the northern state of Punjab, but they live in almost all the major Indian cities.

Due to a series of cultural and social upheavals in the fifteenth century there was a rebellion against idol worship and caste system within Hinduism. Nanak Dev, the founder of Sikh thought, was deeply influenced by these religious questions and began to teach a new spiritual path, the central point of which was the unity and singleness of God.

DO note that Sikhs place the teachings of their ten gurus in their shrine and recite from it. There are no idols here, only religious books.

DON'T forget to cover your head before entering a Sikh temple, the *Gurudwara*. And do eat the rich, oily sweetmeat that is given as the *prasad* or blessing.

DO visit the holiest site of the Sikhs, the 16th century Golden Temple in the northern city of Amritsar for both a lesson in religion and politics. One of the most controversial events in contemporary Sikh history took place when the Indian government at Indira Gandhi's behest, sent in armed troops in 1984 to flush out Sikh terrorist groups hiding inside the temple. You can still see the bullet marks to this day. Indira Gandhi was assassinated by a Sikh gunman, one of her own guards, in part if not in whole to avenge the desecration of the Golden Temple.

DO remember that the Sikhs bore the brunt of the religious violence that followed India's partition and creation of Pakistan. The state of Punjab was divided into two parts and countless Sikhs lost their homes and families in the exodus and riots.

DON'T miss the significance of the five 'k's to male Sikhs. Every true-blue Sikh carries on him the five Ks, the *kirpan* (dagger), *kesh* (Sikh teachings forbid the cutting of hair, the *kesh*), *kanga* (to comb the long hair), *kadha* (a steel bangle and sometimes in gold), and *kachcha* (long, baggy shorts worn as underwear).

DO approach a Sikh if you need directions or are ever in distress or trouble. The chances are very good that he speaks English and that he will keep you from harm.

DO be polite by calling him *Sardarji*. You can also call him *Singh Saheb* or plain Sir.

DO avoid confusion by remembering that a married Sikh couple are not Mr. & Mrs. Singh. He is Mr. Singh and she is Madam Kaur. If you are introducing a Sikh couple to your friends you can say "This is Harjit Singh and his wife Bubbles".

DON'T think that all Sikhs wear a turban and keep a beard. Many younger 'modern' Sikhs wear neither especially those settled outside India.

DO believe your eyes when you see a beard neatly rolled into a hairnet. Letting loose a three feet long beard isn't practical. So many Sikh gentlemen roll their beards into a hairnet the ends of which are devilishly kept in place, under their turbans, somehow...

DON'T get confused by names. Not all Singhs are Sikhs and not all Sikhs use the name Singh. If you have an appointment with a Mr. Singh keep in mind that he might not have a turban and magnificent whiskers.

Christianity

The Christian minority in India are about four percent of the population. The first Christian community was formed around 52 A.D. when one of Christ's Apostles, Thomas, reached India and settled in the southern state of Kerala with a large colony of Syrians. The original converts were mostly upper caste Hindus. Today, their descendants are called Syrian Christians and can still be found in India.

In the 15th century, with the arrival of the Portuguese, Roman Catholicism grew in India.

DO know that the spread of Christianity was much stronger in the south.

DO note that Christian missionaries have struggled to come to terms with the caste system. Most proselytising and conversions have been among the *dalits* 'untouchables' and the indigenous tribal groups.

DON'T think only the poor benefited from Christian missionary work in India. India's middle class has taken advantage of the countless schools run by the missionaries. These are some of the most sought-after educational institutions in India for their standards of excellence. They also teach in English.

CASTE & CLASS

India

Caste

Hindu society is not a great monolith. It has a deeply divided existence, plagued by a 3,000 year old caste system that bedevils the nation even today.

Caste is the most basic social grouping among Hindus. The system, which began as a way of categorizing Hindus according to their occupation, gradually deteriorated into an exploitative and hierarchical order based on a notion of relative purity and impurity.

Every Hindu is ranked at birth as a member of one of four broad castes:

- *Brahmins* at the top: these were the priestly class, said to have emerged from the mouth of the Brahma, the Creator. Before the word *pundit* came to mean an expert, it was the Sanskrit word for a learned Brahmin.

- *Kshatriyas*, or the *Rajputs*, were the warrior class, said to have come out of Brahma's arms.

- *Vaishyas*, the business community, came from Brahma's thighs.

- *Sudras*, the farming and artisan community, from Brahma's feet. They were not considered high caste like the other three.

Relegated to the lowest rung are the outcastes, called 'untouchables', who are regarded as the irredeemably 'polluted'. They were and are to this day, outside the *varna*-caste-system and undertake 'impure' jobs associated with the dead (animal or human) or with excrement. For example, the cobblers who work with leather, sweepers and scavengers (who clean toilets) are considered 'untouchable'.

DO remember that Mahatma Gandhi, the famous crusader of non-violence and considered the father of the nation, strove to liberate 'untouchables' from discrimination. He coined a new term for them, *Harijans* which means 'children of God'. This term is considered patronizing by many today so the modern Hindi word for them, *Dalit*, meaning 'broken people' has more currency.

DON'T think that caste is a thing of the past. Even today, in villages all over India, *Dalit* homes are situated away from upper caste homes. They have separate wells for bathing and drinking water and there is not much social mingling. The marriage of a *Dalit* and non-*Dalit* is still considered shocking and can lead to ostracism or extreme violence. And yes, even in the 21st century, this is true. In many village tea shops, there is what is called a 'two-glass system', one set for the *Dalits* and the other for everybody else.

DO be relieved to know that *Dalits* can enter Hindu temples today. In the first half of the twentieth century, the famous Temple Entry Movement ensured that *Dalits* were not refused entry from Hindu places of worship.

DON'T expect to know a person's caste by just looking at him or her. It is not as simple as race or skin colour. In the cities, the way to find out is by the family name. For example, Sharma is a *Brahmin*; Gupta is a *Vaishya*; Chauhan is a *Kshatriya*; Yadav is a *Sudra*; Jatav or Paswan is a *Dalit*. In the villages, it's the occupation or address that reveals caste. In the cities, economic progress and professional jobs have made social mobility possible for the lower castes. With skill and luck you can be whoever you want to be in the anonymity of a large city.

DON'T even try to aspire for a deeper understanding of the caste system. There are 2,200 sub castes. You'll descend into an endless tizzy. Even the average Indian cannot decipher it fully.

DO be thankful that the Indian constitution guarantees a system of job preferences for the *Dalits* and the indigenous tribes to erase inequalities fostered by the centuries-old system. These job quotas have ensured the presence of many *Dalit* officers in the Indian government and has created a *Dalit* middle class in the cities. In India this is called 'reservation'. Elsewhere it is known as 'positive discrimination'.

DON'T be surprised if someone in India tells you they can manufacture a fake certificate to show you are a *Dalit*. You may wonder why anybody would want to be a 'lower' caste. Job quotas in the government have ensured that in some places this is what you want to be.

DO keep in mind that in the vast arranged marriage bazaar of India, there is no chance of inter-caste marriages. Those villagers who dare to fall in love without finding out their partner's caste in advance, face ostracism or worse. In the cities too, families would initially oppose such matches.

DO believe us when we say that a woman acquires her husband's caste upon marriage. If a Brahmin marries a *Dalit*, she becomes a *Dalit* too. Or vice versa. The children would be known by their father's caste. Sort of like surnames.

DON'T assume that caste is a dirty word in modern India. On the contrary, everybody uses it. Indian politics thrives on it. Political parties brazenly field candidates who would appeal to the dominant castes in the constituency. Political speeches are peppered with appeals to this caste or the other.

DO note that because of the rise of lower castes in Indian politics, the Indian parliament is no longer full of the English-speaking traditional elite who studied at the best overseas universities after they finished throwing out their colonial masters.

DO understand that as a foreigner you do not have a caste identity. You are outside the system and you will be treated as one. If the person you are dealing with is a strict, conservative Brahmin, you will be treated as a beef-eating outsider - not to be touched, not to be allowed into the kitchen because cows are the Hindu mother Goddess, Lakshmi. If you are dealing with a social

wannabe, then you will be treated as a superior caste - someone to be seen with.

DON'T assume that Christians, Sikhs and Muslims in India do not follow the caste system. Although caste is technically a Hindu phenomenon, it is also a social reality. Many Christians, Muslims and Sikhs are lower caste Hindu converts. So even after changing their religion, they are unable to change their social position. The term *Dalit-christian* is self explanatory.

Class

As though caste system wasn't restrictive enough, India has a well entrenched class system. Yes, over and above the caste system. That complicates Indian society like no other society. You could be not just "oh-so-low class", but you could also be "oh-so-low-caste". The interesting thing is that you could be a Brahmin and yet could be low class. It just means you don't have the money, or the right English accent, or no English at all, or fab clothes, or you don't have the right address in the city.

DO know that to be high class in India depends on which school or college you went to. If you are 'convent-educated' or 'public-school educated' it means your parents have the money to send you there. It also means you speak English, uninterrupted by Hindi or words from other Indian languages.

DO look out for those with the IAS tag. This is the privilegenstia. They may not always have the money but those who work in the Indian Administrative Service are the bureaucrats who rule India, the inheritors of the colonial legacy. They are respected, and they also have both clout and connections.

DON'T miss the NRI tag. This is a Non-Resident Indian. Mostly it means those who have family members living abroad (read some rich country, not Bangladesh). The NRI-who-came-back is also high class, gets to frown at the open gutters, and has his nose assaulted by smelly neighbourhoods.

DO note that those who have studied in university in the United Kingdom or the United States are the most pampered lot of all.

DO take heart however, that the biggest thing happening in India is the rise of the middle class, the new money. They are professionals and new first-generation entrepreneurs. They zip around in their tiny red Maruti cars, flash their shiny plastic money and go to the neighbourhood McDonald's. They are very rooted in their Indian culture but prefer to assume non-Indian packaging. They get their fashion tips from watching TV soaps and Bollywood films and their accented English from MTV. Their saving grace is that they are not as concerned about caste as their parents are; and they are patriotic, wanting themselves and India to succeed.

DO look for the rural elite. In villages, the upper caste land-lords are high class. The upwardly mobile *Sudra* castes who found political patronage in the 1990s are the defiant new middle class.

DON'T miss the urban slums. They are the city's lowest rung in the economic ladder and therefore the class ladder. They are home to individuals and families who have left their villages for jobs in the city, or have fled droughts and floods and other natural calamities. They bring with them their rural crafts - the black smithy, locksmith, cobbler, mason and carpenter. Much of the construction work is done by these hard working people and by rural labourers who come to the city for daily wage work. Once they are in the city, they adopt the lifestyle of the city, but in their values they remain conservative.

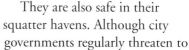

They are also safe in their squatter havens. Although city governments regularly threaten to bulldoze the urban slums, it rarely happens. Not because of compassion. Oh no. It's because the maids, drivers, babysitters, guards and gardeners who make life so pleasant for the rich and upper class, live there.

ACCOMMODATION

India

For the budget traveller

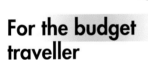

Look for the neighbour hood that screams budget traveller. This is usually situated near the railway station and not the airport. Walk past the loud neon sign boards, down the narrow streets and you'll soon be accosted by men in colourful shirts and dark glasses offering you cheap accommodation in broken English. This is strictly for the low-budgeted backpack traveller who wants value for his money. And forget the luxuries!

DO note, apart from the goats and cobblers, these places are teeming with   tourists, touts and tea stalls. If the hotel offers room service, be polite to the cow roaming outside - that's the milk for your bed tea. But most of these places do not offer room service. You're expected to open your window and shout your order to the tea stall below. It will be delivered to your room. And that is called room service in these parts!

DON'T be shocked, but each ramshackle rest house will have a gaily painted sign outside, proclaiming fancy names such as

Milan International, Dream Palace or at the very least, Neha Intercontinental. These are not international chains. Do not go looking for a branch of Neha hotels in Brussels. The 'international' just means that they're aspiring for international guests.

DO expect just the basics. That's the bed and the four walls with very little space in between. The cheaper ones will have peeling walls dotted with seepage marks. But then at that price, don't expect the Ritz.

DON'T expect a room with a view. Look out of the window and you might get a sight instead of a view. This could be the clutter on the street below or worse, the neighbourhood laundry.

DON'T be offended, but along with the welcome smile, comes a quick businesslike search of your baggage at the reception itself. This is mandatory as the notice on the wall will tell you. In big cities the police has targeted the seedier neighbourhoods as possible terrorist hideouts. Try not to take this too personally.

DO take a look around before you check in. Switch on the television set in the room (if there is one). Upturn the mattresses to check for bedbugs in the lining. Make sure the lights are working. That's it. There is nothing else in the room for you to check.

DON'T forget the bathroom. Opt for the Indian style rather than the western ones. They are easier to clean and are better maintained. And do spray lots of disinfectant before using the loo. Also be wary of using the shower - check the nozzle for rust.

DON'T hand over your valuables to the hotel safe. This is a tricky one. You obviously cannot leave your valuables lying around in the room. On the other hand, can you trust the hotel safe? This is a judgment call. There are no ground rules here. Of course it is safest to carry what you can in a small pouch slung under your shirt.

DO pack mosquito repellent cream and an electric kettle for these hotels. It will make your stay more comfortable. And if you have a problem with the blankets and sheets, bring your own sleeping bag.

DON'T be put off by the dizzying smell of disinfectant mixed with the fragrance of incense sticks. The disinfectant is for you, the incense is for picture of the religious deity hanging on the wall above the check-in counter.

DO explore the neighbourhood to find the cyber café and telephone booth round the corner. You will also see kiosks offering rides to the airport, bus depot or railway stations. This is also where all the touts hang out. It is impossible not to walk down the street and be offered various treats such as budgeted sight seeing and shopping tours. Decline politely. It's cheaper to find your own way around than to trust any of these hackneyed offers.

DON'T just settle for the rough and ready. In the same neighbourhood, you will also get a slightly more upmarket accommodation. Look for the hotel with tinted windows and marbled floors. The extra frills will stretch to cleaner bathrooms, more space in the bedroom between the bed and the walls, television set, telephone and room service. If the hotel offers international call facilities, this will be advertised at the entrance, sometimes in bigger letters than the name of the hotel itself. The accommodation is comfortable, if you discount the slightly musty smell of the blankets.

For the luxury traveller

DO relax. The five star hotels offer a comfortable and somewhat luxurious stay. In touristy towns, do not be embarrassed if you are garlanded when you enter a five star. It's not just for foreigners, even Indian guests are given this traditional, warm welcome. This is the first instalment of several doses of Indian culture that will follow.

DON'T go overboard on those long-distance calls from your five star hotel rooms. It may be easier but could end up being five times the actual charge. Please take the trouble to look for phone booths (advertised as STD and ISD booths) near the hotel that would be open until late into the night.

DO understand that as a foreigner you will have to pay a slightly higher room rate than an Indian. It's called the 'dollar rate'.

DO use your contacts in India to get reduced room rates (yes of course, everything is bargain-able, even at five stars). Indian luxury hotels are the most expensive in the region. Once you check in, you'll wonder why, because they offer fewer facilities than those in Kuala Lumpur, Singapore or Bangkok. Better buy a package tour, because it will work out much cheaper than buying your airline ticket and hotel separately.

DON'T turn down the three stars. These are cheaper than five star hotels but offer clean and comfortable accommodation. Most are situated in upmarket housing estates called 'colonies'. But a word of caution: because they are cheaper, they attract a seedier crowd. If you are a woman alone, avoid the bar in such places.

DO ask for the heritage hotels. Business-minded Maharajas have turned their sprawling and ornate palaces into hotels. They're a heady combination of old world atmosphere with new age luxuries. And a rendezvous with the Maharajah might be thrown in for special effects. That's ethnic India at its best.

DO tip the bellboy, and the room service boys at the hotel. A twenty rupee tip is decent. If you are feeling generous, you could even slip a note into the hands of the burly, moustachioed doorman.

HOME AND HOSPITALITY

India

This is the hallmark of Indian culture. As opposed to the West and the East, Indians would rather invite you home than take you out. It's not economics but tradition. A meal in a restaurant, however fancy, is never enough. You have to be embraced at the Indian hearth and home. And the guest always comes first. There is a reason for this. Indian scriptures tell stories about Gods who disguised themselves as beggars and guests and knocked at your doors. Your karma depended a great deal on the way you treated the visitor who would in time reveal himself and proceed to either bless or curse you.

But a word of caution: if someone invites you to their home without giving you an exact date and time, please do not take the invitation seriously. It's just a conversation piece.

DO be late. Even if you have been given a specific time, be sure to arrive fashionably late. On time, usually means inconveniently early. You may have been invited at the earlier timing but will not be expected till later. Meals are also never served on time. For example, lunch will rarely be served before 2.00pm; even if you have been invited two hours earlier; and dinner will be as late as 9.30pm. By the way, that's early! Usually the drinking goes on till 10.30-11.00pm after which comes dinner.

DON'T despair. The drinks are usually accompanied with lots of heavy snacks. Eventually, when dinner is served, you are either too drunk or too stuffed to appreciate the meal.

DO leave. Please note there is no interval between dinner and dessert. You eat and run. Even if the host politely says "why the hurry?" She is only being polite. An indicator of this is that most Indian homes use after dinner drinks such as Baileys and cognac as an ice cream sweetener rather than a drink to linger over after the dessert.

DO offer to take off your shoes. Take your cue from your hosts' feet. This is not necessarily the person who opens the door. Servants are often barefoot but in some urban homes the host keeps his shoes on. In most houses, particularly the Brahmin household, shoes are taken off before you enter the drawing room. When in doubt, make the gesture. The host might say don't bother removing your shoes, but deep inside he wishes you would. So do remove your shoes and your socks with a whispered, "I prefer to feel your cool floors under my feet".

DON'T go into the kitchen. An Indian kitchen is a strict no-no for beef eaters. A mere whiff of your tainted breath will pollute the entire cooking area. So avoid it. And if you do intrude, then you would be wise to take your shoes off. Usually kitchens also tend to house a small shrine for prayer.

DO bring a gift. They are always welcome. Gauge your host: if he drinks, then a bottle of booze or wine is ideal, but a foreign brand. Although women do drink and smoke, most do so outside the house and almost never in front of their elders. So, avoid cigarettes. If you don't know the host too well, then bear in mind that a bottle of wine can cause a problem if the household has an anti-liquor policy, which may be the case for a Sikh or a Gujarati family or even one from Tamil Nadu down south. Flowers are understood here. So chocolates and flowers are the safest. If there are kids in the house, then target the gift at them. It's the easiest and gets maximum returns.

DON'T go bearing after-shaves to a Sikh household! Perfumes and aftershaves are appreciated unless your host is a turbaned Sikh whose religion bans shaving. If you're staying for an extended period of time, you could occasionally buy some fruit or pastries for the house.

DON'T shake hands with everyone. If someone puts out his or her hand, shake it. If not, fold your hands as if in prayer, bend your head and shoulders slightly and say, *namaskar* or a *namaste*. If you shake a reluctant hand, you'll wish you hadn't, because it will be limp and clammy, like a dead fish. And don't go in for a WWF (World Wrestling Federation) trial of strength. Indian handshakes tend to be more of a hand-rub than a gripping experience.

DO fold both your hands in a *namaste*. In the south, greetings vary from a *vannakam* in Tamil to *namaskaram* in a Brahmin home. But don't bother with the details. *Namaste* has a pan-Indian appeal. If you don't remember *namaste* then fold your hands and say good evening. It'll do nicely. But if you want to earn major brownie points, go for the feet. Touching an older person's feet is the mark of respect. But not if the person is your age.

DON'T kiss hands: is not well understood in India. But if you must, murmur something like "enchanted to meet such a charming lady" as you brush your lips against her hand. You can try shaking hands with a westernised, younger woman but it's advisable to stick to a *namaste* or a good evening.

DO say *"Aunty-ji"*. Call all elders uncle or aunty. And do expect to be called either in return. Young people prefer to use titles and of course, they'll never remember your name. Indians, however, love explaining complicated relationships in the most intricate of details, so you won't be left in the dark about the 'auntie's' exact relationship with your host. Just nod your head and go on calling her aunty. Add a *ji* for extra respect, depending on the degree of grey hair.

DON'T use first names without the *ji*. To play it safe though, if you have to call your host's wife by her first name, add a *ji* to it, such as Namrataji to signify you mean nothing but respect. Otherwise refer to her by her surname: Mrs. Kumar. And **DON'T** be surprised if she refers to her spouse in the third person ("Mr. Kumar") even if he is sitting next to her.

If you see cutlery use it. There are two kinds of homes: western-oriented and traditional. In the latter, you will be served the meal in a *thali* (a large round plate) for your Indian bread along with lots of *katoris* (small metal bowls) for vegetables, meat, curd and so on. The *katoris* will be placed on the *thali* and you use your hand to break the bread and dip it into the food you want to eat. If you have a problem eating with your hands do ask for a spoon. In very traditional homes you may sit on the floor and eat. If in a village, do plan on eating a meal there. You'll sit on the floor and be taken to the backyard to wash your hands before and after the meal.

DON'T use the wrong hand. Do be sure to use your right hand while eating, as the left hand is considered 'unclean'. In fact, when a Brahmin goes to the toilet, he first hitches the holy thread that he wears across his chest over his ears, lest it be contaminated by proximity. So, never offer or eat food with your contaminated left hand.

DO use your fingers. In an urban, westernised home, you will be served at the table, the plates and cutlery will be as you remember them back home, and you may ask for additional implements without offending any sensibilities. But on no account use a knife and fork to cut up the Indian bread - the *naan* or *chapatti* - as both call for a finger job. You will be sniggered at. Most homes offer the basic spoon and fork. Knives come out only at breakfast time.

DO ask for more. Indians eat well and most hostesses do not think a particular dish is a success unless you ask for more. Since the food is usually rich, do use a Delhi-belly (upset stomach) as a valid excuse to avoid overeating. But don't make too much of it, or else the over enthusiastic hostess will rush to the kitchen and prepare a whole new oil-free menu just for you.

DO give your meal preferences in advance. It's not rude. It makes life easier for all concerned. So do tell your hosts if you like spicy food or not. If you're a vegetarian, it's best to inform your hosts, as some houses don't think a meal is complete without a non-vegetarian dish. Such is Indian hospitality, that if a host does not cook meat in the home-kitchen he may order the dish from outside just for you. This rule does not apply in the strictest of vegetarian households, however.

"You hardly ate anything" says your hostess as you sit there stuffed and determined to fast for three days. Pay no attention. She is merely being polite and complimenting you. After all, you know how much you ate. At this point, do touch you stomach with your hand and say that you are really full. Honour will have been satisfied.

DO a discreet burp. If in an urban household, you'll be sniggered at if you burp loudly, regardless of your good intentions. But if in a village, please do a loud burp to indicate how very much you enjoyed the food. You will be smiled at indulgently.

Staying with an Indian family

Although middle class couples now prefer to live on their own, most homes still subscribe to the joint family system. If the family is well off then the older parents have a separate wing but one kitchen, as meals are family bonding time. And whether it's economy or tradition, most homes have an older generation. While the male is the token head of the family, do not underestimate the power of the alpha woman. In fact, do make getting into her good books your first priority because it is she who will ensure your stay is a comfortable one. Also subtly find out about the water, if it's boiled or filtered. Most urban homes have aqua-guards water purification devices. If not, carry your own bottle of mineral water.

Unravelling the joint family

Everyone has a special designation. The brother is a *bhai*. The sister is *didi*. Even grandparents are specified into *dadas* (paternal grandfather) or *nanas* (maternal grandfather). If an aunt is the father's sister, then she is called *bua*. If she is the mother's sister, then that makes her a *mausi*. The mother's brother is a *mamu* while his wife is the *mami*. The father's brother a *cha cha* (like the dance) and his wife is identified as a *cha chi*. There is more, but let's not get into it. And this is only in the north.

DO be confused. The titles vary from state to state. In West Bengal a *bua* is called *pishi,* while in Assam she will be a *pehi.* In Tamil Nadu the aunt is *atthai* and grandparents are *patti* and *thatha.* Even cousins come in specific categories. A first cousin is... But, that's enough. After all, you're not going to settle here.

DO note the special status relationships. The mother-in-law reigns supreme. There's a rather lucrative industry spinning off television soaps based on the volatile mother-in-law/daughter-in-law or the *saas-bahu* relationship. And the turf in question is usually the son. The mother-son relationship is sacred. If you cannot cook a meal the way his mother cooked it, then you haven't won him over! And if there are two sons, the older one's wife holds a senior rank that borders on her becoming a junior mother-in-law. The wife however, has a traditional ally in the *devar* (or the husband's younger brother). In order to work out these subtle nuances all you have to do is go watch a Hindi movie. The clichés are all there in full cinematography and stereo.

DON'T leave your room in a mess. Do make your bed, the first day at least, till you get some feedback. You don't have to dust or sweep the room.

DO leave your bathroom dry. Indian bathrooms do not usually have bathtubs. They may have a shower but a bucket or mug will be provided for your use. You'll also find a plastic stool for repose as you sparingly tip water over yourself. And do remember, there is a water shortage, so **DON'T** leave the taps dripping

DON'T be shocked by the bathroom curios. A curved metal

object faintly resembling sugar tongs may leave you scratching your head. Geographically, you're quite close to the orifice it is intended for. It is, indeed, that curious invention called the tongue scraper. Without doubt you will have heard the hawking, coughing, and spitting which accompanies most Indian early morning ablutions. Some of it, no, lets not be shy, much of it will be due to the gagging which use of the scraper produces in abundant amounts. Why a tongue needs to be scraped is best answered by its followers. Should you feel an urge to experiment, it goes without saying that you should buy your own. Do ask *mausi* or *cha-cha* where they can be bought.

DO carry your own paperwork for the bathroom. Provision for toilet paper varies so it helps to carry your own. Almost certainly however, there is a plastic mug in urban homes, and the rural houses have a curvaceous steel vessel with a spout called a *lota*. If you're in a place where there are no bathrooms, you'll be sent off to the fields with a *lota* in hand.

DO check out how many bathrooms/toilets the home has and divide it by the number of people. That will tell you how long you are welcome in that house.

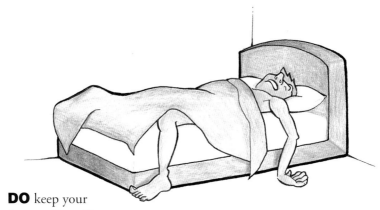

DO keep your
clothes on. Even if you
have been given a separate room, do not sleep in the raw. You'll
shock the servant when he brings the bed tea in the morning. And
do not expect to share a room with an unmarried friend of the
opposite sex. If you are bringing such a 'friend' along, be sure to
warn your host in advance. He may have to brief the elders. Or he
may gently tell you that bringing such a friend is inconvenient.

DO wait on yourself. Most homes have servants to wait on the
family. But the women in the household also help out. So there is
no harm in doing your bit, male or female. You don't have to cook
but you could clear your plate from the dining table to the
sideboard. You will not be expected to wash it.

DON'T forget the servants. As in all cultures, do tip the
servant at the end of the stay. This helps as they usually demand
an extra sum from the host for looking after an additional person.
One hazard with servants is that nothing you do or say in the
house will be a secret. They will spy on you and gossip about you.
So, be cautious what you do in your room. Also, keep your
luggage locked. Keep your money on your body always. Servants
are poor so don't put any temptation their way. But if you like a
servant, it helps to ask him where his village is. It'll make him feel
good.

DO expect lots of tea breaks. Indians drink tea at a moment's notice. The day begins, not with breakfast but *palang chai* (bed tea), which is served while you're still half asleep, sometimes accompanied with a plate of biscuits. This is followed by another cup of tea at breakfast. And if you don't take milk or sugar in your tea, hard luck! In most houses, tea is prepared with all the ingredients thrown together while it's still on the stove.

It's a very sweet, very hot concoction that is served. So if you take your sugar and milk separately, it's best to state that well in advance. And then, hope that someone remembers that and doesn't try to force you to have tea, the 'real way'. This is also often in a glass, rather than a dainty china teacup. Get used to it! If you're visiting down south, it's coffee instead of tea. All other rules remain the same. Coffee is usually served in a steel glass with a round steel *katori* in case you want to cool the coffee by juggling the hot liquid between the two utensils.

DON'T eat too much at breakfast; lunch is only two hours away. The breakfast menu can range from westernised cornflakes, fried eggs and marmalade to a traditional fare of either *idlis* (rice cakes!) or *puri-aloo* (fried bread and potatoes). And two hours later, you will be expected to do justice to an equally sumptuous lunch. Indians don't just feed you. They overfeed you. And still complain that you didn't eat much.

GETTING AROUND

India

The Indian highway

If you have time and are looking for real adventure, try Indian roads. To go to some interior towns, you may have to get down from the 'plane or train and then take a long, dusty, backbreaking journey. The Indian highway journey is like India itself. It is bumpy and has many potholes, it has chaos and cacophony, fast cars and slow cows, adventure and accidents, corruption and economic boom.

DO know that it is cheaper and easier to hire a car with a driver than to rent the car only. The latter option is available, but you don't want to be driving on the Indian highway. They are serious death traps for the uninitiated. You are not after all, trained to dodge bullock carts and camels and oncoming trucks.

DO bring an International Driving Permit from home if you still intend to take on the cows, camels and truck drivers. These come in handy in Goa, where you can rent a motorcycle. You will need to deposit a photocopy of your credit card and passport.

DON'T hesitate to fix a deal with your local taxi stand if you need a car (and driver) at your disposal. His rates will be cheaper than the ones offered by Budget, Hertz and Orix.

DO note that Indians drive on the left side of the road. You're expected to give way to traffic on the right but don't look for such courtesy. On the Indian road, might is right. Don't argue with a truck no matter which side of the road you're on. If a truck honks, make way immediately!

DON'T expect the journey on the Indian highway to be a joyride. It will be a nerve-wracking, death-defying experience. Everybody drives fast and because there are no rules, rashly.

DON'T keep the car windows open in cities. Instead of fresh air, you'll be covered in diesel exhaust.

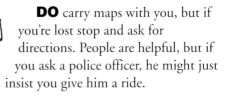

DO carry maps with you, but if you're lost stop and ask for directions. People are helpful, but if you ask a police officer, he might just insist you give him a ride.

DO get ready for more potholes than road. Although India has one of the largest road networks in the world, it is poorly maintained. Potholes not only make the ride bumpy but also slow you down.

DON'T miss the rural India that passes you by. Indian highways are rarely barren and boring. You will see farming and bazaar activity on the way. The entire rural enterprise is on display, from the blacksmith to the herbal remedy for impotence, from the *desi* (country) liquor shop to the highway prostitute, from the hand-woven bamboo basket to the fly-infested milk sweets. Don't miss the turbaned farmers and their veiled wives.

DO learn to choose your *dhaba* food. *Dhaba* is a rustic highway restaurant. All you have is a kitchen and a few cots on the dirt. The food will smell great and you will be very hungry. But look around for the restaurant that truck drivers hang out in. These are guys who go back and forth every day and they wouldn't eat at a place that gives them an upset stomach.

DO choose an Indian car if you have to go on a long journey into the Indian hinterland. The sturdy and stalwart car is the Ambassador, an ungainly bubble modelled on the 1953 British Morris Oxford: it's slow but reliable. Everybody on the road understands this rather simple car and its parts are available at every tea stall even in the middle of nowhere. The joke is that even a child of six can fix it with chewing gum as an adhesive. Which means the Ambassador is the car for you. No fancy, fragile foreign cars for the Indian road.

DON'T think of hitch hiking unless you are really desperate and have absolutely no other option. This is not safe, not even for Indians. There is plenty of cheap public transport to choose from.

DON'T miss the signs on the trucks and the buses. They'll vary from nonsensical message such as 'OK Tata' to *'Pappu ki Savari'* (*Pappu* is a common Punjabi pet name and *savari* means ride!) to dire threats not to caste your evil eye on the truck! Another common sight is to see a bunch of green chillies strung like fairy lights across the truck, or sometimes shoes hanging from the rear bumper. That incidentally is for good luck. The idea is if you appreciate the beauty of the truck too much, it brings bad luck. So a shoe contributes to the ugliness of the vehicle.

DO observe the crowd that gathers around a railway crossing. You will be stopped when a wooden bar guarding the tracks is lowered. Every vehicle will stop, except the bicycle, the scooter and the motorcycle. The drivers on these vehicles will just bend and crane their neck under the wooden bar and peddle right through the tracks. The guard will patiently watch and not stop them.

Meanwhile those of you whose vehicles are not lower than the wooden bar can choose from an array of food that is presented to you at the junction to while away your time - freshly cut radishes, carrots, tender coconuts and sugarcane.

DO enjoy the variety on the narrow Indian highway. From camels to cows. Bands of children and goats will suddenly appear out of nowhere. A bullock-cart, a tractor, a truck, an elephant, a cycle, car and a bus - all jostling for a narrow ten yard strip of bumpy road.

DO get used to the loud noise of vehicles blowing horns. That's one way of letting the other daring and possibly drunk driver know that he cannot bully you on the road. So it's actually a good thing.

DO be warned that the cacophony could give you a severe headache. Drivers live on their horns. On the highway, you even hear a whole variety of horn-tunes, ranging from the regular to the musical to the cuckoo bird horns. Noise pollution in cities varies. Bombay is quieter than Delhi.

DO notice that in the countryside, farmers will position their rice husk straight from their harvest onto the road. They expect you to drive over their grain as it helps remove the husk more easily.

DO call your family and friends if you take a long journey on the highway. There are a number of yellow and black coloured STD and ISD booths (long distance call facility) on the road. It'd be good if you call your folks every couple of hours and inform them that you are doing alright and where you are.

DO note that there are no toilets on the Indian highway. On the other hand, the entire highway and the farmland is a giant toilet.

DON'T hesitate to get down and walk over to a bush or a tree and squat. That's the only way.

DON'T panic if you see carcasses of smashed trucks in the exact position of the accident. The police discourage drivers from moving their trucks from the site of the crash as it might disturb official investigation. So, the drivers of the truck camp next to the wreckage for days for fear their unattended cargo may be looted by bandits. And cause incorrigible traffic jams in the process.

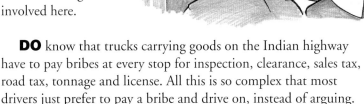

DON'T expect the traffic jam to open up within minutes. It could take hours sometimes, as fragile 'truck-driver ego' are involved here.

DO know that trucks carrying goods on the Indian highway have to pay bribes at every stop for inspection, clearance, sales tax, road tax, tonnage and license. All this is so complex that most drivers just prefer to pay a bribe and drive on, instead of arguing.

DON'T stop if you hit a cow. It's better to run for your life. Remember the holy cow is one of the most auspicious symbols in Hinduism. A cow is worshipped as the mother of humanity. If you hit a person and if you have a conscience, then just run to the nearest police station and turn yourself in. If you stay on the road, the surging crowd will turn on you.

Bus

DON'T take city buses. They are crowded and there is real risk of your pockets being picked. But do note that the buses in Mumbai are more user friendly than those in Delhi which have been known as 'killer buses' for good reason.

DO opt for the window seat if you clamber onto an empty bus. It will soon fill up and then standing passengers leans towards the seated ones and breathe heavily on their faces. If you climb onto a crowded bus, then God help you. You will be pushed and pulled and groped all over, regardless of your sex. The worst is you're never sure if the aggravator is feeling you on purpose or if he is being pushed in the general direction of your private parts!

DO take the inter-city buses. And try the luxury buses, which means air conditioning and Rexene seats with loud, garish Hindi movies shown on a small jumpy television. Curtains made of coarse cloth are another bonus for the 'luxury' traveller.

DON'T however, expect a toilet in the bus. A few luxury coaches, affiliated to five star hotels may offer one, but as a rule there is no such provision. But there will be frequent stops on the road: if you're in a luxury bus the stop will be at a roadside restaurant. If you're travelling cheap, then you'll just have to visit the fields.

DO sit up front, near the engine and diagonally across from the driver's seat. The view is much better through the bus windscreen than the dirt smeared windows with 'safety glass' printed on them.

Autos and cabs

DO insist on paying by the meter. The auto is three-wheeled public transport. It is also called auto-rickshaw in India.

Both the auto-rickshaw and cab drivers will try and fleece you by first insisting that the meter is not working. Don't believe this story. What further complicates your chances of getting a fair deal is that the amount on the meter is never the actual sum. This sum is then checked against a fare-chart (because of the frequent diesel and petrol  hikes, it's easier to print a new chart than change the meter). Insist on seeing the chart yourself. Don't take his word for it. The chart is usually complicated but pretend to understand it.

DON'T expect electronic meters in small towns. It's advisable to first fix the price and then get into the vehicle. He may still charge you a high rate but at least he won't take you for a site-seeing tour before reaching your destination.

DO expect to pay extra if the cab is air-conditioned. Mumbai has blue coloured 'cool cabs' that are more expensive than the regular ones. And in Delhi, don't be surprised if every other cab driver is a turbaned Sikh. In Delhi and Mumbai there are some air-conditioned buses on limited routes.

Rickshaw

DO try the cycle rickshaw, a regular feature in small towns and old quarters of cities. This is a small carriage pulled by a man on a bicycle or a man on foot. Slow but quaint. And in some places, the only way to travel. You may feel bad for the puller but remember, this is the way he feeds his family. So don't hesitate to take the ride.

DO opt for a cycle-rickshaw for a leisurely and inexpensive tour of a provincial town. You can hire it for the entire day. But

remember to fix the price beforehand and when you stop for tea and lunch, don't forget that the thirsty work is done by your (usually ancient) cycle-wallah. So include him in.

The great Indian train journey

If you have the time and want to travel the way the teeming millions do, then try the train. It gives you a glimpse of India in a way that nothing else can. The great Indian middle class travel from north to south for 48 hours with the entire Hindu Undivided Joint Family and packed food. They carry their household and their kitchen with them. They will change into their nightclothes, carry make-up, towels, extra pair of slippers and chessboards too!

Steam engines have been phased out in India. The majority of Indian trains run on diesel. Suburban trains tend to be electric. Trains between big cities and towns are connected by broad gauge.

DO take care you don't step on people coiled up on the floor of the railway platforms. India's platforms serve as homes for the homeless of the city. There are hundreds who use the platforms as a dwelling for bathing, eating and sleeping. Some of them are also people who have travelled from villages and have onward journeys to make. Since they cannot afford hotels, they sleep on the platforms. Or they live on the platform until tickets are available.

DON'T think the platform is only about poverty. For years, a red-haired Indian princess, the Begum of Oudh, parked herself in the capital's railway waiting room as a protest against the British Empire who deposed her ancestor way back in 1856. She sat majestically on a Persian carpet in a dark room without running

water or electricity, dictating letters of protest to Queen Elizabeth and the Indian prime minister. She has since been persuaded to take residence in a bungalow in the city.

DO note that the old kingdom may have moved out, but new money is everywhere at the station. Railway stations in India are the centre of entrepreneurship and economic activity. The little *chai* (tea) shop, the cigarette shop, the suitcase handle-fixing shop, bookshop, cobblers, shoeshine boys... The Indian bazaar is out there. Many important Indian towns have traditionally developed along railway stations on the basis of railway activity, for example Mughalsarai (in Uttar Pradesh), Arakonam (in Tamil Nadu), Kharakpur (in West Bengal).

DO be careful when you travel by trains. Crime is high, theft of baggage and pickpockets are common. Thieves lurk around railway yards and break into wagons carrying goods too.

DON'T accept food, water or juice from strangers, even if they are co-travellers. This is a common way to knock you out and rob you while you are still unconscious. One is called the Biscuit Gang and they offer drugged biscuits to unsuspecting travellers.

DO protect your luggage. At the platforms, chains with lock and key are available. You can chain your suitcase to the hooks under your berths.

DO buy inflated rubber pillows at the station if you need a comfortable headrest during your journey. If you have forgotten toothbrush, toothpaste, comb or soap you can buy them at the station. If, however, you're travelling air-conditioned class, you can get a pillow, blanket and clean sheets on board.

DON'T panic if your ticket says RAC. It means Reservation Against Confirmation, waitlisted. This is not a confirmed ticket, but you can board the train with it. You will not get an entire berth, but you will get space to sit and travel. The main guy to contact for confirmation and for berth is the TC, the Ticket Checker.

DO look for the TC. He usually enjoys 'demi-God' status in the saga of train journeys. He is the most sought after personage. He is that 'black coat white pants' guy. He is the answer to all your ticket problems. You will see him surrounded by a mob of desperate and anxious ticket seekers. If you have trouble with your co-passenger, contact the TC, he will get you a safer berth elsewhere.

DON'T pull the chain unless you have an absolutely good reason to. You will be fined five hundred rupees.

DON'T struggle with heavy baggage yourself. You can use the coolie. They are the porters in red shirts on railway platforms. Highly unionised, the coolies are the largest manual

workforce in the world. They carry the load on their head and they are what was euphemistically called 'baggage assistance' in the First World War. There are no baggage restrictions. The coolies can also get your tickets confirmed for an extra tip. And do bargain with the coolie.

Once you have boarded the train for a long journey, get ready to make new friends.

DON'T mind the barrage of questions coming from your co-passengers. They are as perplexed as you are at the prospect of a long and lonely journey. They will strike up a conversation, borrow your newspapers and magazines, offer to share their homemade food and pickles. They will want to exchange addresses and telephone numbers. Use your own discretion on how friendly you want to be.

DON'T drink liquor on the train. If you do, hide it well.

DON'T expect food on all trains. Only on long journeys, overnight trains, or the super fast trains like the Rajdhani and Shatabdi trains will food be served. In the super fast trains, the cost of the ticket includes food. Veg and Non-Veg options are available. But almost every station sells cooked food or packed biscuits, bread and eggs.

DO weigh yourself on the giant weighing machine at the platform and also get your day's fortune told. The weight may not always be right but the fortune may just be. If for nothing else, you might enjoy its Wordsworth-ian English. A typical card may read: Your day will be like a sunflower, bright and radiant.

DON'T try too hard trying to follow every word of the platform announcements. It is never clearly audible and you are better off asking the coolie, who is better informed.

DON'T trust the platform tap water as it may ruin your journey. Buy bottled mineral water, preferably outside the station as in smaller stations the bottled water have fake seals and are not safe.

DO use the cloakrooms available in all major stations to store your luggage for over a month for a small fee. There are safe deposit lockers at some stations. There are rules about the weight of luggage that can be stored in the cloak rooms/lockers. Lock and secure your luggage of course.

DO note that you don't have to wait on the platform if your train is late or if you have time to kill between two trains. You can rest in the retiring rooms available on the platform.

DON'T forget that there are at least eight classes of accommodation in Indian trains. 1st Class AC Sleeper Car (this is the best needless to say, there is a bathroom too and cabins that you can lock. Best if you need privacy, but it costs as much as an air ticket). AC 2 Tier Sleeper Car, AC 3 Tier Sleeper Car (both these are the most preferred by the middle class; berths are separated by curtains, therefore little privacy). AC Chair Car (best for short trips), First Class Ordinary (no AC, no privacy), Sleeper Class Ordinary (chances of theft high, a lot of passengers with unconfirmed seats will push you about), Chair Car Ordinary and General Class Ordinary (forget it, this is not for you).

DON'T expect to find tickets whenever you show up at the counter. You have to book them in advance. A week to ten days is sufficient. Remember, this is the way India travels, so tickets get sold out easily.

DO look for the separate queues for foreigners at the booking counters. Special tourism centres in the heart of some cities also accept reservations so you can save a trip all the way to the smelly station.

DO know that Indian trains have separate 'ladies only' compartments. If you are a woman travelling by yourself and are nervous, this is a good option. But this may mean that there are too many wailing infants with their new mothers, if you can tolerate that.

DO make sure you have tickets for all the sectors of your journey. You get a separate ticket for each time you change train or direction.

DO note that Indian railways have a computerized reservation system in most of the big cities and towns. Master and Visa credit cards are accepted in most locations.

DO buy the Indrail Passes, which is meant only for foreign tourists or Indians living abroad. It lets you buy journeys for point-to-point travel without route or train restrictions including on the super fast Rajdhani and Shatabdi Express trains within the period of validity. You have to pay in dollars or pounds sterling. It neither saves you money nor a visit to the booking counter. It works only if you are planning extensive rail travel.

DO remember you have to fill out a form before you buy the ticket. Details about your name, address, age, sex, the name and the number of the train, and your destination are asked for. If you cancel the ticket 24 hours before the date of departure, you will be penalized a nominal amount. Otherwise only sixty percent is reimbursed.

DO always insist on getting the upper berth if you don't want to be disturbed by co-passengers. It is also safer for your luggage. Choose the inside berth instead of the outside berth. The latter is too small and you will be disturbed by people walking back and forth.

DO note that there is a discount on tickets for senior travellers (women over 60 and men over 65). You must show your passport to verify your age. You can pay by your credit card only in big cities. When you pay cash, only rupees accepted.

DON'T buy tickets with berth numbers 1 to 8 and 65 to 72, as they are next to the noisy, smelly toilet area.

DO remember that if an unused ticket without reservation is presented up to 3 hours after the departure of the train, a refund is possible with a nominal deduction. The scale of deduction is different for the different classes of reserved tickets. No cancellation charges shall be levied on RAC/wait-listed tickets. No claim for refund is entertained in the case of lost or misplaced or torn tickets.

DO ask the stationmaster or coolie for the exact location of your coach when you arrive. It is not easy to climb on to any coach and move towards the one you want.

DO get used to the stink from the toilet. Do wake up early enough to beat the queue and ensuing smell.

DON'T expect an announcement about your destination. Most trains do not inform you where you are. Your ticket will indicate the time of arrival in the city of your destination. But the train could be late. So the trick is to tip the boy who brings tea or bedding and ask him to inform you about your destination. Or even the TC. Or just keep asking everybody around you.

DON'T look out the window at the crack of dawn because the tracks are used as loos by the residents living in shanty towns along the tracks. You may be in for a surprise if you are hoping to catch some fresh breeze or a glimpse of sunrise.

In cities like Bombay and Calcutta trains are the best way to get around. But be prepared to jostle with the crowds, cheek-to-cheek, butt-to-butt. And take care of your wallet. For the incorrigible ticket-less travellers there is an informal but innovative insurance scheme that takes care of you when you are caught. But you are advised to buy the ticket. In the evenings it is a common sight to see women cutting vegetables for their evening meal in the train on their way home from work.

DON'T miss out on the thousands of aluminium lunch boxes that Bombay trains are famous for. This is cheap, home-cooked food that is delivered to factory workers and professionals all over the city. Each dabba or box is marked with the name of the factory, street address and employee codes.

DO travel by the Palace On Wheels, if you have the time, inclination and above all the money. This is a luxury five-star hotel on wheels and takes you through exotic desert locales in Rajasthan. Ask your travel agent for information. It is recommended for those whose priority is not to befriend the average Indian. You are likely to find only foreigners or rich Indian honeymooners on board. In Gujarat, the luxury train is called the Orient Express.

Air Travel

This could be the way the moneyed travel in India but it has its own share of quintessential Indian idiosyncrasies. Until 1992, there was only one national airline, run by the government and known for its sluggish monopoly. While things have improved drastically with the entry of a number of private airlines, the airport ritual continues to be cumbersome and bureaucratic. Here is a quick list of mantras to remember.

International flights

DON'T expect a scenic view outside the airport. Air travel in India may be for the well heeled, but airports like the one in Mumbai sit right in the midst of a sprawling slum. Again, such things are typical in India.

DO enter your mobile phone or laptop on the 'Tourist Baggage Re-Export' form at the time of arrival if you're planning to take it back with you. Otherwise you'll be accused of selling it in the black market. Unless that is your intention! If you're bringing a high priced electronic item, go through the Red Channel. Otherwise it's the Green Channel for you.

DON'T carry more than USD10,000. Otherwise you'll have to declare it. Why bring so much money? India is not an expensive country. And when we last checked, the Taj Mahal was not for sale.

DON'T pay any FT (Foreign Travel Tax) on international tickets at arrival or departure. The amount has already been paid at the time you bought the ticket and will be marked on your ticket as FT.

DO ignore the lines of people sleeping on the pavement or in the waiting lounge of the international airport. It's not unlike a railway station. They are either turbaned Sikhs waiting for a ticket to join their relatives in Southall and Vancouver, or else Haj pilgrims sleeping on the airport floor awaiting their flight. Since most do not have a confirmed ticket, they often spend days camping at the airport, sleeping bags and grandmothers in tow.

DO notice that when a relative returns home, it's treated as the grand return of the native son. The entire joint family shows up to receive him with flowers. Sometimes neighbours do too. This is why the waiting lounge looks more crowded than it should.

DON'T try arguing with an airport trolley. It has a mind of its own and will move in one direction as you push it in another. Just count yourself lucky that you've got one as these are often in short supply. But you have no good reason to complain as they are free of cost.

DO be prepared for an instant crash course in the great Indian queue in front of bored, scruffy-looking Immigration officials.

This could take a while, not because the officials are tough with their queries, but they are slow. This is followed by another wait and a chaotic jostling routine near the conveyor belt at the baggage claim. It does get a little better once you step outside, but not much!

DON'T be surprised if the toilets stink, especially the ones at the Mumbai and Kolkota international airports. But if you're in Delhi the situation is much better. Often the first impression of India is a strong smell of bathroom stink. Quickly look up your tour guides and reassure yourselves that there is so much more this country has to offer!

DON'T leave for the airport without your tax clearance certificate if your stay extends more than 120 days. This is to ensure that you have been spending enough foreign currency and have not financed your trip by earning money in India. It's a mere formality - go to the tax department in any of the four metros with your bank exchange receipts and you'll get it. You're not always asked for it, but it's safer to have one.

Domestic

DO note that all foreign tourists pay a higher dollar fare for air travel within India. Well, that's one way of levelling the rate of exchange that favours dollars over rupees! And international credit cards are accepted.

DON'T worry, there is no cancellation fee on a dollar ticket for internal travel. You also don't need your passport to book a domestic flight.

DO however pay the security tax for domestic travel. Ever since September 11, all airlines charge an additional security tax. For travel within India this works out to USD5 per sector. This is added to your ticket price and paid at the time of buying it. In fact, most travel agents add this to the price when they quote a fare. And before you feel discriminated against, Indians pay it too.

DO give your local phone number at the time of booking. This could be to your travel agent or the airline office - whoever your booking agent is. As flight delays are common, some airlines do call and inform you ahead of time. So you can enjoy that extra hour of sleep. If you haven't got that call, then phone the airport before leaving to ensure your flight is on time.

Okay, so now you have bought your ticket and are ready to check-in. **DO** be prepared for some serious frisking. First the cops will search you and then, just before you board the plane, the airline officials will do a body search. So, there are two body searches.

DO be prepared to open all over again that hand baggage that just zipped up with a great deal of hard work. Before you board the plane, they make you open your hand baggage and rummage through it in full public view. They open even wallets, toilet bags, soap boxes. But nobody helps you stuff it back again.

DON'T take that bonsai plant onto the plane. The security drill is fairly tight. And for some reason the plant is a serious threat. As are lighters and batteries. Mobile phones and laptops are allowed on board but phones have to be switched off.

DON'T expect luxury at the economy lounge. You'll have to make do with peeling walls and rows of plastic chairs. In smaller towns, buy your cup of coffee before you proceed for the check-in. There will be no vending machines or food stalls inside. And if you're eating at the airport restaurant, expect airline food at inflated prices. The cheese sandwiches will have more butter than cheese and the coffee will be lukewarm.

DON'T forget to identify your checked-in baggage before you board the flight. There are no signs for it, you just have to be alert to the announcements. Once you have identified your luggage, a tag is stuck to it and only those are thrown into the plane.

DON'T expect the airport in small towns such as Raipur in Madhya Pradesh or Jammu to be more than a landing strip with a small building attached to it. And when you leave the building, don't look for fancy cabs. Sometimes, you will get nothing more than a cycle rickshaw. That's India with all its contradictions!

DO note that there are cabs and buses that take you to and from the airport. But there are a few simple rules to keep in mind.

DO look out for the pre-paid taxi service when you land. Delhi airport has two such counters: one is manned by the local police and offers a reasonable rate. There is, however, another counter, handled by Delhi tourism. Both booths are placed strategically near the entrance. If you're an economy traveller, then look for the one that has the Delhi traffic police sign. In this case, do trust the police!

DO take the air-conditioned option if you can afford it. The queues are minimal at the Delhi Tourism counter. These air-conditioned luxury vehicles are private cabs. They'll even offer to carry your luggage and escort you to the waiting cab instead of letting you struggle with the trolley as you go out looking for your cab. Of course, all this comes with a luxury price tag. But if you can afford it, then head for this counter.

DON'T get confused by the ITDC (India Tourism) booths at other city airports. These work on the same principles as the Delhi Tourism booths. So, if you're on a budget, go out and take one of the cabs or autos waiting outside. You'll still be fleeced but it'll be cheaper.

DON'T hesitate to ask the price before jumping into a non-prepaid cab. Most cab drivers will quote a price above the meter. You can look to a loitering policeman for help, but it's wiser to check with a fellow passenger and then bargain. If it helps, even local Indians end up paying the extra fare as the cab driver knows there are limited options from the airport. Ditto for autos rickshaws (the three wheel taxis).

DO look for the airport bus if you're on that kind of a budget. International airports offer a bus ride to the city's central point at half hourly intervals during the day. If you arrive in the middle of the night (most continental flights land at this hour) and don't have accommodation booked, its wiser to wait in the airport's air-conditioned lounge for the 6am bus. Otherwise you're at the mercy of the cab driver and his exorbitant night charges.

HOW TO BEHAVE
IN PUBLIC

India

Working on the assumption that you are a responsible adult who knows how to behave with a modicum of decency and restraint, we won't impose too many restrictions on you. In other words, these rules are for a person who won't talk loudly in public spaces, will not point fingers at strangers and not use abusive language. Is that asking for too much?

DON'T litter. There is no law against it but that doesn't mean you should. If you look hard enough you'll find a dustbin amongst all the sea of orange peels, plastic wrappers and cigarette stubs lying on the road. The Indian mindset is that one more scrap of paper won't hurt.

DON'T neck in public: Public displays of affection, even with your spouse, should be restricted to the bare minimum (no puns here, please!). Shady bushes in public parks are used as a cover by

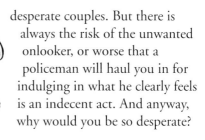

desperate couples. But there is always the risk of the unwanted onlooker, or worse that a policeman will haul you in for indulging in what he clearly feels is an indecent act. And anyway, why would you be so desperate?

DO dress modestly. Men in sleeveless Tshirts and torn jeans are often mistaken for hippies and treated accordingly. Women should dress decently (short skirts and tight tops are indecent), otherwise this will be seen as an invitation to ogle. And perhaps more. So every time you visit a public place pretend as if you're going out in the company of your very conservative grandmother and you'll behave just right.

DON'T buy from street vendors. You'll be offered very cheap and exotic smelling food by vendors strolling around the public park. Avoid it. For sure he has not used mineral water in their preparation.

DON'T walk over a person even if he is lying in front of you and blocking your way. It's easier to jump over him but it's also considered inauspicious. If he notices he'll make you jump right back to undo the damage done. So in the long run, it saves time to walk around the hurdle in front of you.

DON'T rush to the police if you see child labour at the local restaurant. Although it is illegal, it is tolerated and even justified in the name of helping the poor. You may tip the child or buy him candy.

DON'T step on a book or a newspaper or a magazine. Every written word is considered to be sacred by the Hindus who worship Saraswati, Goddess of Knowledge. It is sacrilege to touch it with your feet. If you do so accidentally, then touch the book to your forehead. And all will be forgiven.

DO note the writing on the wall. Indians have discovered a shortcut to immortality by scribbling their names on walls that could belong to public bathrooms or ancient monuments. The literature varies from declarations of love (Bitoo loves Pinky forever) to obscene. One memorable message on an overpass in south Delhi a few years ago was *Jesus Is Coming*. To which somebody had thoughtfully added: *To become a Hindu!*

DO avoid the touts and tour guides. But in some places such as public monuments, they are a necessary evil. There is rarely any comprehensive literature available, so it helps to have a local explain all the colourful legends to you. Otherwise it's just another old monument. The trick is to fix the sum in advance so he doesn't fleece you for an exorbitant amount later. The guides, who are often old codgers, know so much that you'll be swooning with an overdose of history and anecdotes.

EATING OUT

India

If you eat Indian food, you probably think chicken tikka masala and Madhur Jaffrey if you are British, or banana leaf curry if you are from Southeast Asia. But travel one hundred miles in any direction and you will find food that is not served in any Indian restaurant in your town.

Like the Indian people and their languages, their food reflects where they are, who their ancestors were and what their caste is, and which God or Goddess they venerate. So as with China, their food is categorized by region.

Gujarati food for example is rich in vegetarian dishes, often sweetened with sugar even if it's a vegetable curry. Andhra Pradesh food is rich with aromatic spices in the tradition of the Nizam of Hyderabad's kitchens. West Bengal cuisine, because of its many rivers, is a treasure trove of fish recipes. While its vegetable curries often carry the signature flavour of *panchphoran*, a mix of five spices unique to the region. In the south, curries in coconut milk, prawns and sea fish mark this region out as dependent on the oceans for food and livelihood.

As you travel this huge country, do be adventurous. Eat the local dishes, discover vegetables you have never seen before, sample the mangoes (the best in the world), savour the tang of curries laced with tamarind, and devour India's sugar-laden desserts. And if you like what you eat, do buy a cookbook to experiment on your friends back home.

Eating out

The range varies from five star hotels to roadside cafés (*dhabas*). But the etiquette remains the same. Be polite, be patient because as a rule, Indian cuisine takes time to prepare. And don't hesitate to ask the ingredients of a dish you cannot fathom.

DO be polite. Snapping your fingers is frowned upon. You could, however, catch the waiter's attention by waving your hand sideways, not unlike a car wiper. Or else beckon him as you would a small child: fingers moving against your palm in a downward motion and a smile on your face. If you have to call out, call him *bhaiya* (brother). But not in fancy restaurants.

BLAH. BLAH.
BLAH. BLAH. BLAH
BLAH. BLAH. BLAH
BLAH. BLAH. BLAH BLAH
BLAH BLAH......

DON'T speak rapid English: At non-five star restaurants, the waiters have a working knowledge of the language which does not exceed the menu and phrases such as 'thank you' and 'have a good day'. So try not to engage him in a lengthy discourse.

DO tip. At fancy places, ten per cent of the tab is the expected norm. But if the bill is very high then use your discretion. At roadside *dhabas*, even loose change is appreciated. Rs10 will go a long way, especially as the bill rarely exceeds Rs100.

DON'T go dutch. As a rule the one who invites, plays the host and picks up the tab. While Indians don't go dutch, a common habit amongst friends is to take turns at paying the bill. But if you have done the inviting, then you are expected to pay - even if your guests are Indians. And always offer to pay when you are with a woman! A little chivalry is well appreciated.

DO clap when the live band at the restaurant plays your favourite song. Most times, the musicians make more noise than music but that's because they're treated as stereos rather than human beings. Most guests tend to ignore the band. If you clap, you'll be noticed for your courtesy. And that's never a bad thing. The risk is they might continue singing for two more hours instead of packing up.

DO you want lots of coffee, or just a cup? Here's a tip. When ordering coffee, ask for cappuccino, which will come by the cup. However, if you've ordered regular coffee, please insist that you want one cup only. Otherwise you may get stuck with a whole pot!

DON'T expect hushed silence. Meals are boisterous occasions, unless of course it's a working lunch. So, don't cringe if loud laughter drifts across the room. This is particularly true of five star coffee shops where the table next to you will probably have a crowd of college youngsters, a group of housewives or maybe even a family gathering. No use complaining. The poor maitre d' can do nothing about it.

Liquor timings

There are strict deadlines for serving liquor and these vary in different cities. In Delhi the pubs take their last order at 11.30pm and in the five star bars it is 12.45am. In Mumbai the deadline is 11pm.

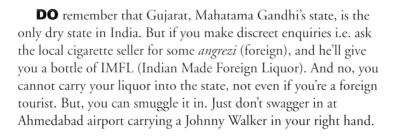

DON'T despair. Remember, you're in India where rules are meant to be broken. A small bribe can ensure you get beer served to you in innocuous looking teacups. Just don't add any sugar to it.

DO remember that Gujarat, Mahatama Gandhi's state, is the only dry state in India. But if you make discreet enquiries i.e. ask the local cigarette seller for some *angrezi* (foreign), and he'll give you a bottle of IMFL (Indian Made Foreign Liquor). And no, you cannot carry your liquor into the state, not even if you're a foreign tourist. But, you can smuggle it in. Just don't swagger in at Ahmedabad airport carrying a Johnny Walker in your right hand.

DON'T share a *thali* (platter). Usually *thali* is meant for only one person and you will be frowned upon if share it. Same advice applies if you go for the buffet.

DO ask around for the better (and safer?) restaurants when in a strange city. And no, don't try the Web even if you are in a relatively upmarket city like Hyderabad. It won't help. What you could do is to ask the hotel desk or better still, local shopkeepers to guide you.

DON'T say "mild" if you can't eat spicy food. Say "NO SPICE". People in India don't understand "mild" the way others around the world do.

DON'T mistake the small bowl of lukewarm water with a slice of lime that is served after an Indian meal. It is not lemonade for you to drink. It is a fingerbowl for you to refresh your hands after picking at your tandoori chicken.

DO note that after every Indian meal, you will be served a mix of sugar and aniseed (*saunf*). It is a digestive, so do try it. Another popular after dinner aide is the paan. This is a leafy triangle containing amongst other gooey stuff, some betel nut. It's a digestive. Don't bite into it like a sandwich. Stuff the entire concoction into your mouth and let the juices flow. Red stained lips are a casualty.

DON'T expect Chinese food to taste like Chinese food. Indian Chinese is a separate genre by itself as it is spicy and cooked with Indian herbs. Because it is laced with chilli, Chinese restaurants often market their food as Szechuan style, the region in China famous for its spicy food. Of course, a Chinese from that region wouldn't recognize what he is served in India!

Roadside cafés

DO ask for mineral water, but you are not likely to find it. Instead quench your thirst with a bottled soft drink. If he does have mineral water see that he breaks the seal in front of you.

DO be careful and avoid unpeeled raw vegetables and fruit. Meat should always be ordered well done.

DON'T look askance if your yoghurt or *lassi* (combination of yoghurt and water and very cooling in the summer) has a greenish tinge. It hasn't got mildew. *Khas* (sweet smelling grass) has been added to give it a flavour and for its cooling effect.

DO be suspicious if you are offered non-vegetarian dishes at ridiculously cheap prices. Chances are instead of mutton or chicken, you'll be served something less than the chicken you ordered. And no, you don't want to take a guess!

DON'T get too excited if the sign at the roadside café says: Chic-Inn. It's not serving chicks. Just badly spelt chicken.

DO make a beeline for the stall that has a lot of truck drivers as its customers. Regulars on the roads, they know the café that offers the best fare. Try the *daal-makhani* (lentil with a chunk of butter), hot *naan* (Indian bread) and the inevitable tandoori chicken, also known as the national bird of India. As a side dish, you will be served onion rings with a green coloured mint paste. Eat the onions, avoid the paste. It's very chilli.

DON'T forget to round off the meal with a cup of tea. Well, cup is only figuratively speaking. Unless specified otherwise, tea will be served in a glass. It will be milky, very sweet, flavoured with cardamom. Try it, it's an acquired taste.

DO ask for a straw when you order a fizzy, bottled soft drink, as the mouth of the bottle could have a rusted cap.

Street food

DON'T try this if you have a weak stomach. But if you like spicy food with a difference, this is a must. Mumbai is famous for its *bhel-puri* on the Juhu beach. It's a combination of puffed rice with onion and green chilli and drenched in tamarind paste.

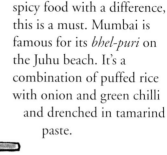

DO the *paani-puri* (flour based balls filled with spicy *imli* (tamarind) juice). The more cautious insist on Bisleri water being used for the juice, others add vodka for that extra zing.

DON'T try the fried stuff however much you may be tempted by their delicious aromas. The *samosas* (puff pastry pyramids filled with potatoes) and *pakoras* (vegetables cooked in flour batter) may smell seductive. But they've been fried and re-heated at such regular intervals that they're saturated with oil; Mobil oil at that! If you want to eat fried stuff, go to a restaurant.

Desserts & sweets

DO opt for the Indian fare. The *jalebi* (round orange squiggles) are very famous in north India. Eat these while they're hot and crisp especially on a rainy day. It's both a celebration of the Indian monsoon and the palette. Lentil based, the centre is filled with very sweet, sugar syrup.

The east is famous for its desserts: milky *rasmalai* and *rasgullahs*, white round balls floating in sugar syrup, all made from reduced milk. Most Indian sweets are a combination of reduced milk or cottage cheese with lots of sugar, pistachio and cashew nuts added for taste.

DON'T worry if your *burfi* (fudge like milk sweet) comes in wafer thin silver foil. The silver is good for you and meant to be eaten. It won't hurt your insides. It will however stick to your teeth so you may want to rinse your mouth afterwards.

DO ask for *kulfi*, the Indian version of ice cream which comes with sweet noodles and rose flavoured syrup. It gives Hagen Daaz a run for its money! Apart from which some local Indian brands offer rich creamy ice creams, such as Vadilal in Gujarat or Milk-food in Delhi. Ask your local friend to point you in the right direction. This is important. There are as many cons as there are success stories. So be careful and don't eat ice cream that is spelt Quality instead of Kwality. Believe us, it's not the quality you want!

Feeling homesick

DO look for some old familiar signs in the big cities and you'll see McDonald's, Domino and Pizza Hut. But with a difference.

DON'T ask for beef burgers. You won't get McDonald's famous beef burger here. One look around at the cows

Old wives' tales about food

DO drink this for a sore throat: honey, hot water and turmeric powder (*haldi*) with a dash of brandy. Yes, you'd rather have the brandy but apparently it's the *haldi* that does the trick.

DO kill pain with hot milk and turmeric powder before you go to bed. This works as a good pain reliever if you fall down and hurt yourself.

DON'T worry about the strong odour: eating raw onions also has a cooling effect in the summer heat. You'll stink but you won't have heat stroke. Also try roasted oats, ground and mixed with water and sugar. A glass of this concoction also has a cooling effect - it works for horses, so why not for you?

DO take care, you may be pregnant. If you ask for anything sour, especially if you're a young woman, be prepared for knowing smirks. The general perception is that pregnancy brings on a craving for sour pickle, unripe mangoes, fresh tamarind and lime.

DON'T know how to cope with high cholesterol? No, we are not asking you to pop some pills. Try *methi* (fenugreek). It is supposed to reduce blood glucose and cholesterol.

DON'T lose your day if you have an upset stomach. Take a bowl of plain yoghurt, add two spoons of *methi* seeds and swallow the mixture. You can do this two or three times a day depending on your need.

DO stay away from tea if you want to remain fair and lovely. They say too much tea makes you dark skinned. Now you know India is a dark skinned nation, it's all that in-between *chais* that they keep gulping down.

DO rub mustard oil on your toes and chest on cold nights. It will give you an enveloping warmth. But it might leave you cold as far as human company goes, thanks to the smell.

DO eat ten *tulsi* (basil) leaves every morning with water for 108 days if you want a long life. The *tulsi* plant is worshipped by Hindus and almost every traditional village home has a plant in the courtyard.

DO look for pomegranate seed and bark if you want a child. Hot water with the powder of the seed and the bark cures infertility. If you have sagging breasts, then mix *neem* oil (margosa leaves) with powdered pomegranate rind and boil it, cool it and massage onto your bosoms. Either way the pomegranate is a woman's best friend.

DON'T overeat the hot, spicy food. You might get mouth ulcers. And if you do, take powdered *aamla* (Indian gooseberry) with honey.

loitering on the road outside and you'll know why. In fact, even the lamb burgers are not meeting with much success as there is a great deal of suspicion about the kind of non-veg served by a foreign food chain.

DO look for the chilli burgers. Bland fast food has been adapted and spiced up to suit the Indian palette. And the McAloo tikki burger!

DON'T hesitate to try the Indian fast food joints. You get potato filled vegetable burgers, *chicken-tikka* (pieces of chicken) burgers and even mutton wrapped up in rolls of *roti* (Indian bread). Or just opt for *puri-aloo* (round-shaped wheat, fried and served with potatoes). In the south you could have *idlis* (steamed rice cakes). That's the Indian fast food menu. And it works.

ENTERTAINMENT

India

Indians have very few avenues for public entertainment. Going to the movies is universal. Going to the local park for a stroll with the family in the evening is also common. Plays are for the culture vulture. In the southern city of Bangalore, the big thing is to go to the pubs. In Bombay, it is going to the beach and eating out. In the villages, it is still the local folk singer and the puppet shows and those who do the rope trick in fairs. There are also the performing monkeys and bears and snake charmers in smaller towns.

Bollywood

You cannot imagine India without its movies. It is the only real popular culture we have. It is the world's largest film industry, churning out more than 900 films a year. Typically, a Bollywood potboiler *masala* movie is a heady concoction of melodrama, song and dance extravaganza. You can dismiss it, but you would be wise to look for lessons about India in it.

DO make it a point to go watch a movie while you are in India. It'll give you a glimpse of the Indian melodrama. Every movie has at least six songs thrown in between scenes of romance and histrionics. There are predictable and simplistic plots - the boy-meets-girl love story, the revenge theme and the odd social issue. The teeming millions mired in poverty and chaos, want their movies to offer unreal, escapist fantasies. It offers an alter-life for them.

DON'T expect consistency either. The male and female characters, even if they are poor can suddenly take off and begin dancing in the lush green meadows of Switzerland. Switzerland is where every Indian thinks paradise is.

DON'T expect the men and women to wear the same clothes throughout the song.

For decades, Bollywood shied away from showing the kiss. Instead it would show two birds, or a bee on a flower bud. But things changed in the early 90s and the movies became more daring. But by and large our cinema still remains the custodian of Indian middle class values.

DON'T get shocked when you see women doing hip jerks and the men planting a kiss on their heroine's navels, but fighting shy of kissing on the lips. Indians are still prudish when it comes to kissing. But there could be a wet sari scene where a rain drenched heroine gyrates to erotic lyrics in her damp clinging sari. In the very next scene she may be covered head to toe being the dutiful and demure Indian virgin.

DO expect stock, black and white characters because an Indian film is usually a morality play. The flawless hero, the coy heroine, the sadistic villain... The good always wins. And it is usually a happy ending.

DO expect to see a lot of crying by characters in the movie. It's melodrama, mega scale!

Indians love the Lost and Found themes. There are countless movies made on how three brothers get separated in crowds and wander their whole life searching for each other. Their mother is usually blind and cannot recognize them. But two and a half hours later, in a miraculous twist she regains her sight and identifies the little birthmark on her son's body. The mother in Indian movies is a repository of all virtues. She weeps silently throughout the film, and usually sacrifices everything for her son who in turn reveres her like a goddess.

DO follow the music soundtrack of the movie even if you don't understand the lyrics. The songs are the best part of the film and may make more money than the film itself. And don't be shocked to find that even horror films have songs.

Movie stars are gods too

The biggest and the most famous icon of Bollywood is Amitabh Bachchan, who played the role of the angry young man to the hilt through the 70s and the 80s. When he was battling for his life after an accident whilst filming, the entire nation plunged into grief and prayer. Indians idolise their stars.

DON'T be surprised when you hear of temples built for movie stars where they are worshipped with religious fervour.

DO note that chief ministers of two Indian states in the south were former matinée idols. One even used to address election speeches wearing the (religious) costumes of his movie roles. Film stars are also wheeled out of their tinsel world into the grime and dirt of Indian elections for campaigning. They are big crowd-pullers.

Going to the cinema

DO keep in mind that a number of moviegoers are just couples who want to neck and kiss in the cinema halls in the back rows. Just ignore them. It reflects the lack of privacy and space in a country of a billion.

DO be warned that Indian films do not usually have English subtitles. But it shouldn't matter too much. You can still follow the story.

DON'T always expect to get tickets when you show up. They are often bought in bulk by profiteers who sell them to desperate punters at twice the going rate. If you don't get the tickets at the counter, try the parking lot attendant or the cigarette shopkeeper next to the hall and he will lead you to a tout who holds the stock of tickets.

PSSST

HOUSE FULL

DO take earplugs. Cinema halls usually play the films really loud.

DO hand your ticket to the man with the torch and he will usher you to your numbered seat.

DO give yourself a good three hours for the film. This is probably why the seats often slide back so you can take a snooze or get really comfortable for the inevitable melodrama. There is usually an intermission just when you are getting hooked on the storyline.

DON'T lose your temper if people around you talk throughout the movie. In fact people talk, cheer, clap and whistle too. Movies are the Super Bowl of entertainment in India.

DO be tolerant towards people who bring infants to the movies. The wail that you hear may not always come from the screen. It could be the child next to you.

DON'T expect Hollywood movies to have subtitles when they play in India. People understand English in the cities. Or if they don't, they don't really care; they just go to watch the action scenes.

Other entertainment - when cinema is not an option

DON'T look too puzzled if Indians around you break out into a chain of tuneless singing. This is a game called *Antakshari*, based on Bollywood songs. It's not for you as you're not a true-blue Bollywood fan who knows the lyrics of every film song. The trick is to sing a song that begins with the last letter of the song your opponent has just sung. No singing prowess is needed here.

DO switch on the television to get a wide and dizzying range of all that's Indian and then again, not quite: religious chanting to MTV; from long drawn out cricket matches to the WWF; Baywatch babes to soaps about dutiful Indian daughters-in-laws battling their evil mother-in-laws; Hindu epics to Oprah Winfrey shows. TV is the entertainment centre of Indian homes along with the ubiquitous VCR. Cable

TV has changed everything and now there is something for everyone in the joint, undivided Hindu family. Brand new Bollywood movies are brought into the homes illegally within a day, thanks to the black market encouraged by the local cable-wallah.

DON'T get startled when the man next to you suddenly jumps up and yells "OUT"! Just look carefully, he might be holding a tiny transistor close to his ear. He is listening to cricket commentary, the great Indian male pastime.

For Indian spice - try newspapers

True to the democratic strain, India takes the notion of a free press very seriously. Sometimes, the politicians would say, Indian media is too free. The lack of strong defamation laws also adds to this freedom.

DO know that when it comes to Hindu-Muslim riots, Indian media reports tend to exercise a lot of self control. Newspapers will present all the details - number of dead, injured and the causes for example. But they carefully avoid using the words Hindu and Muslim. Don't be surprised to see a sentence like, 'Members of one community clashed with another'. It's for you to draw your own conclusions. Mentioning who is fighting is considered provocative as the authorities fear it will lead to more rioting in this large, multi religious country. But TV has changed all that. It is now hard to hide the religious identities of the rioters and the victims.

DON'T expect scandals exposing the personal lives of politicians. That is strictly off limits. You would never find a Monica Lewinsky-type scandal in the Indian media. But expect plenty of corruption scandals.

Indian newspapers are obsessed with politics - a by-product of democracy again. As a visitor you don't need to follow every detail, unless you want to be entertained.

WOMEN TRAVELLERS

India

If you are a single woman traveller in India there is one word for you: Caution. You could be winked at, touched, brushed against or groped. But that shouldn't put India off your itinerary. With a few simple tips you can stay safe and still have fun.

DO always wear your backpack on your front with your elbows sticking right out. That way you guard the contents of your bag and also protect your breasts from unwanted attention.

DON'T bother rushing to the police station if a man follows you. This is normal. Just avoid eye contact with him, look for a busy street, stop at a teashop or go into a store and chat with people. That is enough to scare him away.

DO note the Indian male has a lot of stereotype about foreigners - "Easy". He has grown up in a segregated society, watching lusty Hindi movies, totally dominated by mother and married to a woman chosen by his parents.

DON'T touch, try not to shake hands, always fold your hands and say *namaste* whenever you are not sure about an over friendly man. That way you look respectful and decent, but also avoid touching people you don't want to.

DON'T sleep with him on your first date. If you do like an Indian male and want to date him, wait till he asks you out.

DON'T go to bed with the guy on the first date - or even on a second or third date. Be sure of your own feelings and what you may be getting into.

DO insist he uses protection. India has the largest number of HIV-infected people in the world, more than South Africa. The government estimates are 5 million HIV-positive Indians. But both India and Indians are in denial about the reality of AIDS. They still think this is what foreigners have brought in!

DO ask a local friend about safe touristy spots. If you are in a place that's buzzing with tourists, you are okay. You can go for a boat ride in Varanasi, on a cycle rickshaw to view the Taj by moonlight in Agra, or to the beach in Goa. But if you're not sure, better stay indoors or at least close to your hotel.

DO note that some cities are safer than others. Bombay is safer than Delhi for women. People are too busy in Bombay to notice who is doing what. It gives you anonymity. Calcutta is safe for women, but there is not much nightlife there. Bangalore, the pub-city, has a nightlife that is fairly safe, but it's still better if you have company. Go with a local if you can.

DO rest assured that a single woman can have a drink without being considered easy, and in a restaurant of repute. If you are single in the evening, your biggest problem could be transport back to your hotel. Taxis will fleece you by taking you all over the city. So it's always better to book a taxi and keep it with you

throughout the evening, or rely on a friend. And forget Chennai (Madras). It has no nightlife unless you have a local friend who can take you to some discos or five-star hotel bars. The pub-city, Bangalore is also safe for a single woman who wants a drink without being considered easy. But if you are in small towns or villages, stay indoors.

If you are a smoker

DON'T worry about it in the big cities. Although it is still rare to see ladies with a fag in their mouth, it is acceptable. Most women do not smoke in the presence of elders as a mark of respect. In small towns and villages, you will be stared at, no matter what you do. So why bother holding back?

DON'T call it sexual harassment, it is a benign, lukewarm term: 'eve-teasing'. Remember, if you are whistled at, touched, followed, stared at, there is nothing you can do about it. Even if you are touched, it is not called sexual harassment. There are laws that protect you against eve-teasing, but nobody ever bothers to complain. Indian women just live with it. But if you do go to a police station, the cops will help you if it's not night time and if you are modestly dressed. But generally, if you were in a busy place, bystanders would help if you call out in distress.

Going to the movies

DO go for a movie in the evening. It's safe to go to the big cinemas halls, which are usually crowded. Just ensure you have fixed your transport back to your hotel in advance.

DON'T show those long shapely legs. That doesn't mean you have to act as if the Taliban police the streets. Just don't wear minis or tight clothes. If you are on a Goan beach, anything goes. The same is true for Kovalam beach. But if you are in the north, take care not to show too much skin. Sleeveless shirts are fine. Sarongs are fine. Bermuda shorts are fine during the daytime. But always carry a scarf if you are wearing spaghetti straps.

DO try wearing Indian clothes. A sari is the Indian national dress. It has six yards of fabric, that you wrap around yourself. You need a lot of practice to carry it off. Only make your street debut if you are very sure it won't unravel. Otherwise, admire yourself in the comfort of your room. When you arrive in India you may wonder why there is all this fuss about dressing modestly when Indian women wear saris that reveal their entire midriff, their navel, and sometimes even their cleavage! The thinking is: it's okay if it's a sari. But showing legs and thighs is what will invite lecherous looks!

DO also consider the *salwar kameez* if you are looking for comfortable Indian wear. It is originally a north Indian attire. It covers everything and is safe. It is like wearing pyjamas and a long shirt over the top. But the smartest thing would be to buy fabric (India is rich in this and you can find wonderful bargains) and have western clothes made out of them. Bring your favourite clothes to have them copied.

DON'T sit with the men. At parties, take your cue from the Indian women. In the more traditional families, the chiffon clad women sit separately sipping soft drinks while the men gather around a bar and talk loudly. You can join them, they look like they're having more fun. But then you may be considered 'too forward'. And in India, that's not a nice label.

DON'T always count on the police. In fact try and stay as far away from them as possible. The low level constables are the worst. They tend to be crude and even lewd. But if you have to report theft or cheating, go with a trusted Indian friend if you can. Or with your travel agent. An agent will in all probability know the ins and outs of the 'How to bribe the police and get work done' routine.

DO show a lot of deference to the police. To a male police constable, quickly call him a brother or *bhai*, before you explain your problem, in the hope of preventing any lecherous advances that he might entertain.

DO bribe discreetly if you have to. Don't ask for a receipt. The euphemism that the north Indians prefer to use is "*Mithai* for the kids". It means the cop or the official wants your money to buy sweets for his children.

DO look for the Ladies seats in public buses. You can ask a man to vacate it for you. There are exclusive Ladies Compartments in trains. If you are travelling alone, ask about it when you book the ticket.

DON'T worry about toiletries, except when you head for the villages. India stocks a wide and high quality range of toiletries and cosmetics. This includes international brands but priced much higher than the local ones! **DO** try out the local herbal and *ayurvedic* cosmetics and creams. Some big towns also stock disposable diapers and you get sanitary napkins at every local chemist or general store. Except of course, when you're headed out to the villages. In which case, pack everything from your toothbrush to the lipstick.

DO try the *itar*. This is the local perfume. It is not alcohol based but oil based and tries to capture the essence of flowers. The variety ranges from jasmine and rose to sandalwood. A word of caution: the preparation is oily so be careful not to smear it on your clothes. It could leave a stain. *Itar* is easy to carry and makes an ideal gift for friends back home.

TIPS FOR MEN:
DON'T RUSH IN

India

This is a survival guide for the male in you. Though Indians make a lot of allowances for foreigners, that is not true when it concerns their womenfolk. The local village belle may look easy prey but she is probably watched by an army of male relatives.

DO beware of touts and con men who promise you an evening of pleasure. They presume that you are loaded and are looking for women. It may not always be safe, let alone pleasurable.

DO make it a point to accompany an Indian host when you go out partying. Or, stick to the more expensive side of town. You may go looking for a bargain at the seedy bars and end up paying a lot more!

DON'T try the direct approach. Virtue is an old fashioned word and India is an old fashioned country at heart. Indian women are raised to be virtuous. They will protect their virtue vigorously, and so will their men-folk. Gauge the woman well, before you approach her. Be doubly cautious of rural women or women from small towns. You will hear stories of mistresses, wife swapping and other interesting things in the cities, but trust us, this is not for you.

DO always remember that dating is a concept understood and practiced by very few of the upwardly mobile urbanites. An Indian lass can face a lot of social disapproval for going out with a foreigner.

DON'T indulge in unprotected sex. There are sex workers but it is an illegal trade and they are not necessarily AIDS-free. This is not the souvenir you want to take home to your wife or girlfriend, so be careful. Indian sex workers do not carry medical cards.

DON'T over-estimate your charm. Don't take an acceptance of your dinner invitation as an evening of sex. The maximum you should go for on a first date is a kiss on the cheek. As it is, Indians tend to think foreigners are too fast. So, whatever you do, don't hurry that impression. It won't get you your second date. Unless of course the woman indicates otherwise. But as a rule, if a woman drinks and smokes, it does not mean it's a signal for casual sex.

DO pay. However independent and modern the Indian girl may seem, she would still like her date to pull back her chair, open the door and pick up the tab. She may offer to go dutch, but if you really want a long term relationship (i.e. a second date!), do pay the entire bill.

Ditto for the men. If you've been invited out, then the host pays the entire bill. There is no concept of sharing the cost.

Similarly, if you extend the invitation, then you are expected to clear the check. Credit cards work in cities but carry cash in small towns.

DON'T do drugs. Being invited to an evening of drugs and drinks could end up with you losing all your cash and clothes. Yes, India has its share of con men and con women. Drugs are illegal and there are frequent police raids.

DO be well dressed. Appropriate clean clothes, good manners and demeanour go a long way. The preppy look is always in. If you're dressed in torn jeans and sleeveless Tshirts you may be mistaken for a hippie with all its connotations, and treated as such.

DO go to discos. Apart from being very hip and fun, it's a good place to meet a dancing partner. Ditto for five star hotel bars. If a girl is alone, so much the better. She's probably there looking for male company. Yes, this also happens. But if she is with a guy, then be sure to talk to him first. That way it won't look as if you are hitting on the girl - even if that is your intention.

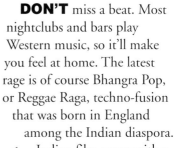

DON'T miss a beat. Most nightclubs and bars play Western music, so it'll make you feel at home. The latest rage is of course Bhangra Pop, or Reggae Raga, techno-fusion that was born in England among the Indian diaspora. Indian film songs with a western beat are also popular. Just flow with the rhythm even if you can't follow the lyrics.

DO go to the pubs if you are in Bangalore or Mumbai. They're very trendy and cheaper than the large hotels. They're the favourite watering hole for India's brat pack. Delhi is still to catch on to the concept of a place where you go to have a drink, listen to music and relax.

DON'T drink the local brew. Avoid shady joints, their alcohol may be home-made *tharra* and you could wind up in a hospital or seriously dead. Foreign brands of alcohol are available and some good quality Indian brands, including some fine wines. You can always purchase yours from a licensed liquor store. Don't go for cheap bargains.

DON'T think that every time you see men holding hands, they're gay. They are often just good friends. It's okay for men to hold hands and walk around. In fact, in rural India it's a much more common sight than a man and a woman holding hands in public.

DON'T, however, come out of the closet in a hurry. India is still to give a public seal of approval to homosexuality. There are no gay bars, but in some big cities like Delhi, five star hotels and some discos have gay nights. For example, only gays and lesbians allowed on Thursday. So, make that discreet pass, but only on your day of the week!

DON'T carry too much cash. Be very wary of pickpockets, especially in crowded bars and discos. It's wiser to spread the risk and divide the money in two pockets. And avoid the wallet. In a crowded street, all it takes is for someone to jostle against you and minutes later you'll discover you've been relieved of your cash and cards. Wear a pouch next to your skin, under your shirt.

DO check your bill. More so if you are tipsy. The bill could include drinks that you haven't consumed. But if you are in a particularly seedy tavern, it's advisable to pay the inflated amount than get into an argument as there will probably be some muscle-flexing guy on the premises, ready to rough you up.

DON'T believe she loves you at first sight. The Indian tradition frowns on promiscuity. Good girls are those who take their time before showing their love. So be very wary of a local girl who claims to love you, too soon too fast. She is probably looking for a green card out of this country, or at best, a holiday in India, at your expense.

DO tip. The general rule is ten percent of the tab. But Indians are not generous when it comes to tipping. In roadside hotels and seedy cafes, Rs 10 is enough. You don't have to tip the cab or auto driver. He is probably charging you an inflated fare in the first place by pretending his meter does not work. Also, in hotels, tip the bellboy when he carries your bags. After that, it's up to you if you want to tip room service or not. If you have hired a local guide, you could tip him or better still give him a present at the end of your trip.

SHOPPING

India

Do shop: ecstasy now

Shopping in India is a religious experience - it elevates the soul, frees the mind, lifts your spirits and it suits every pocket. What hits you is the sheer variety. The fabrics and colours, gems, jewellery, semi-precious stones, artefacts, handicrafts. You can even get handmade footware.

DO enjoy the variety. Shopping can vary - from the flea market-type vendors on the streets, to shopping malls. So take your pick. And don't miss the street bazaars. Every locality has a selected day of the week, when in the evening vendors will suddenly appear en-masse with goods piled on carts or set up on the pavements and then come nightfall, they fold their wares and vanish into the night. Needless to say, exercise caution as far as the quality of goods is concerned.

But what the hell, they are so cheap anyway!

DO be warned, every shop will quote a different price. There is no such thing as standard pricing or standard quality. Each item has its own distinct pattern unless it's the uniformity of a branded label. And window shopping is understood here. The shopkeeper has all the time in the world, so make the most of it.

DO bargain as it is a national sport next only to cricket and strikes. Bargaining is an art. You casually browse around keeping your expression neutral. Don't have the frenzied look of "I gotta have it!" Then you place the item you want on the side and ask the price of a few items you are not interested in.

DON'T ever pay the price you're asked. It's a game that is played both by the shopkeeper and the customer. The haggling is

part of the fun. So do raise your eyebrows when the price is quoted - it doesn't matter even if you've done a quick foreign exchange calculation in your mind and discovered you're paying half the price you'd pay back home. You are expected to frown and shake your head, sadly.

DO remember that there is an unlisted *gora* (white skin)-tax. All shopkeepers mark up their goods by 200 percent when they see a foreigner, regardless of the colour of his skin. In fact, even Indians with a slight accent get gypped.

DO ask for a discount. It doesn't matter if the goods are neatly tagged, you can still get the price knocked down. Don't feel sheepish. The shopkeeper expects you to ask and has already kept that margin in mind when he marked his goods. Even branded, electronic stuff is negotiable.

DO try the pavement shops. But when you do, roll up your sleeves and start haggling. This is serious business and the shopkeeper will probably be disappointed if you take him at his word and pay his inflated price. He is looking for a round of serious bargaining, so oblige him. But make sure you do a thorough check of the product before you pay.

DON'T ever laugh at his broken English as he asks "what much"? And do smile at his not so subtle attempts at flattery: "Madam will look just like Lady Diana in this dress," even though you look a tad like Imelda Marcos. The poor man is only trying to earn his living.

DON'T buy trash. There are state emporiums in every state capital that stock the specialty of their state. You will find all the exotica imaginable there. Usually the price is non-negotiable, but don't let that stop you from asking for a discount. If you think you are going to travel to different cities, ask around for what the city is famous for. For example, Jaipur is known for fabric, blue pottery and semi-precious stones; Varanasi is known for silk and carpets.

DON'T buy a Lacoste shirt or Nike shoes at pavement stalls. They may be attractive at half the price, but they are likely to be fakes.

DON'T ask for your money back. You can exchange goods if you're not happy. But you will not be reimbursed. Even if it's a big department store. You can however pick up something else from that shop at the equivalent value.

DON'T buy silver and gold from the small shops on the roadside. The shopkeeper will swear by all his ancestors it's genuine, but trust us, it ain't. Even if the shop is air conditioned with the jewellery displayed in glass cases it always helps to check with your local Indian friend to direct you to reputed shops. Also do be warned: if you ask for a receipt, you will then be told that he has to raise the price for "tax purposes." Now what do you do?

DO know your carats. Indians prefer gold ornaments of 24 carats purity, but 18 carat gold ornaments are also available. Do remember that any gold with studded gems, real or semi-precious, will be in 18 carat. Don't get charged for 24 carat gold price. Look knowledgeable.

DO ask about opening hours as most shops close by dusk. Neighbourhood shopping areas usually have a weekly day off and not all shops close on the same day. Ask before you visit.

DON'T expect to be able to shop well into the night. Shopkeepers have families too and like to get home early to dangle their kids on their knee. However, many shops are open on Sunday in case you feel the need for even more retail therapy.

RURAL INDIA

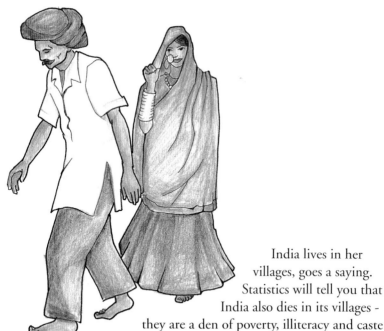

India lives in her villages, goes a saying. Statistics will tell you that India also dies in its villages - they are a den of poverty, illiteracy and caste divides. But this is also where India's soul and culture thrives. For the villager, the city is a place of sin and greed. For the city person, the village is about charm and simplicity. Both notions are wrong.

In the typical Indian village, homes will be segregated along caste lines. The upper caste landlord's house will be big and at the centre of the village with a well, a hand pump and even a school. Not easy to find too many of these in the lower caste quarters.

DO notice that the villagers dress differently than the urban folks. The old men will be in *dhotis* (white wrap-around cloth) and turbans. The women will be wearing saris, but may wear it a little differently than her sisters in the cities. The village women also wear a lot of ethnic jewellery. The women in the northern villages cover their head, and sometimes veil their face as well. Not so in the south. Some women may have tattoos on their faces or limbs.

DON'T be taken aback by the excitement you will generate in the village the moment you arrive. If it's a remote and poor village, your car will be an exotic sight. Groups of noisy children will follow you everywhere. The women will shyly peep out from behind closed doors.

DO head straight to the house of the village headman. If he okays you then the village will accept you. This could be an elected chief of the village council or the biggest landlord. If you just visit the lower caste homes, the landlords may be offended. You have to pay your respects to them.

DON'T think the villager is all that different from his urban counterpart. But yes, the packaging is different. Despite the clearly impoverished status, the warmth and hospitality is much more genuine than in the city.

DON'T worry about the children who will run after you and giggle when you turn around. You're an outsider in a place where there is no circus, no cable TV. So you're the official entertainment. Get used to it. **DO** remember that they're not being rude. They're actually being friendly. Wave at them, smile and pull their hair - gently.

DO oblige by taking a few pictures if you have a camera. The villagers love it, no matter how old they are. They all want to be photographed, even though they may never see the prints. The women will be a little shy, but will join the throng once they know you don't mean any harm. Their demands to pose will be many. So if you are running out of film, just keep faking. They wouldn't get to know.

DO note you will be offered water and tea immediately. Just point to your bottled mineral water and politely decline. If they insist, just tell them your bottle contains medicines and you can't drink any other water.

DON'T be discourteous. If they have already made tea for you and you don't want to drink it, then just do a mock-sip and nurse it for an hour. As the tea contains boiled water this will not be a digestive risk. But it will be very sweet and very milky. And it will be served in a glass. **DON'T** expect the villager to pull out cups, saucers and saccharine sachets!

DO look for the most learned in the village if you have language problems. It is usually the schoolteacher who could help you with translation. But to break the ice, do fold your hands and say *"namaste"*, until the teacher comes.

DO remember if you are travelling with a partner of the opposite sex, introduce him/her as your spouse. They will approve instantly.

DON'T be intimidated by the crowd even if it seems to be an invasion of privacy. Learn to ignore the curious hanger-ons who will follow you around. If you want to have a serious chat with one person, it is next to impossible, as there will be at least two dozen people eavesdropping. **DON'T** shoo them away as they'll soon be back.

DON'T try too hard to strike up a conversation with a woman if she seems reluctant and shy. You may have to speak to the men in her house before they let you speak to her. **DO** be careful, even your most innocuous question can be misinterpreted as a come on.

DON'T cringe if they hand you an infant whose nose is flowing and looks dirty. The proud parents will feel offended.

DON'T ask for the dining table. Meals are eaten on the floor. The women will not eat with the men but will hover around and serve them. That's the way it is. And yes, you'll just have to sit cross-legged on the floor like the rest of them. At the very best, you may be given a cushion. The food will be spicy and very healthy. As a rule, the villager economizes on cooking oil. However do carry your digestive pills and you may find the change of water (used in cooking) hard on your stomach.

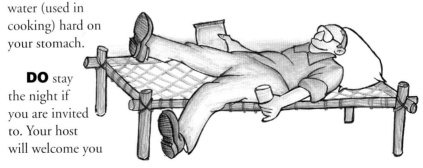

DO stay the night if you are invited to. Your host will welcome you and give you his best *charpoy* (matted cot) to sleep on. But what do you do about the mosquitoes that have a knack for sniffing out fresh blood? Just carry lots of mosquito repellent and hope for the best. **DO** carry your sleeping bag in case you think you will get rashes from unwashed sheets.

DON'T look for the attached bathroom: The toilet, if there is one, will be far away from the sleeping quarters. It may at best be a squat-toilet. A hole in the ground with two bricks placed on the side. You are supposed to balance on the bricks and squat over the hole. And please, don't fall in. A word of caution: empty your pockets before you try this acrobatic feat. You don't want your keys or wallet to slip into the hole, do you?

DO go to the field for your morning rituals if you prefer. Many villages do not have even the squat-toilet. If they do, it may be very smelly and fly-infested. It's much better if you just wake early enough and walk with a mug/bottle of water (not toilet roll, as you don't want to litter the place) to the farmland.

DON'T hesitate to follow the man in a hurry who will be carrying a *lota* (steel curved vessel) as he heads for the nearest field. Choose a nice bush, look left and right and then squat. **DON'T** strike up a conversation with another villager doing the same. Ignore the cows as they walk past. After all, they've seen it all before.

DO take your radio with you if you want to stay in touch with the rest of the world. Many villages may not have a television set, although this is slowly changing.

DO ride the bullock cart or tractor if offered. If there is a local fair going on, arrive in style in the local bullock cart.

DO carry lots of pencils to distribute to the village children if you think you are going to spend time there. These are inexpensive gifts and will go a long way for making quick friends with the little ones who will guide you all day around the village.

The village chic in urban India

In cities like Delhi, there is another village that is very different from the villages that you have just visited. This is village chic, the imagined village. The best example of how impoverished villages along the city's edge have become trendy hot spots, is Delhi's Hauz Khas village. It's a perfect example of how a few fashion designers, gourmets and interior decorators got together to open some of the most expensive shops and galleries in the dusty lanes of this old village.

There will be an odd cow and an old moustachioed man gurgling at his water pipe. But this is part of the chic, fashionable look of the complex.

DON'T mistake this for the real Indian village. It is a frozen relic that has been re-packaged for the city's elites.

DO go to a farm party. No, this is not a harvesting festival. The ultra rich have farmhouses tucked away on the outskirts of big cities. These are lavish Italian marble complexes replete with landscaped lawns, golf courses and swimming pools. Do not look for turnips and tractors here. The lavish parties may end up with you and your fellow revellers diving into the pool, clothes and all.

INDIAN MARRIAGES

India

Made in heaven, arranged by parents

Fair, good looking, wheatish complexion, homely, adaptable, cultured veg family, well placed family, caste no bar, high income, talented, unencumbered, own house, issueless innocent divorcee, preparing to go abroad, only son, all sisters married, farming business, no liability, willing to settle in the US, status family, send full length photo, charming, convented girl, no dowry, decent marriage, income in five figures, diploma electronic working in MNC, traditional values, good features, H1Bvisa, green card holder, send biodata, mark sheet, sub caste no bar, girl only consideration, settled rajput radiologist boy, modern outlook with traditional values.

Sounds like gibberish? This is how Indians marry. They wash all their prejudice, fears and greed in public in the classified pages, Sunday after Sunday, in national and local newspapers. In the maze of these words, you see an India that is changing and one that is obstinate. Of course also the one that hasn't quite made up its mind which way to go.

DO note that each time the name of the caste is flaunted in a marriage ad, they are looking for a match from the same caste. This is India at its inflexible worst. In villages, if you dare to fall in love outside your caste, you could be beheaded, stoned or driven out. In the cities, they are subtler about their disapproval.

DON'T think when they say 'no dowry' they want nothing at all. They often mean there will not be a list of demands handed to the bride's parents. Or they are just trying to say they are not the bride-burning kind of folks. This does not necessarily mean the girl's family go scot-free. They still have to summon up all their life's savings to give jewellery, car, cash...anything they can.

DON'T be deceived by the word 'decent'. Decent marriage means the boy's parents are not going to ask for dowry specifically but they do expect you to spend a decent amount of money at least, so that their social prestige doesn't take a tumble.

DON'T think 'homely' is a negative word. It does not mean plain. It means somebody who would serve her husband and his family dutifully and unquestioningly and prefers to be a housewife.

DON'T be surprised at the large number of ads wanting cultured and traditional women. It just means that they expect the girl to touch the in-laws' feet and cook at home. Her priority better be the husband and his family, even if she has other interests and a high-powered and demanding job.

DON'T be mistaken that they only want 19th century brides. They often say they want 'Convented girl' which means someone who speaks good English, who is smart and is intelligent. And if she is working and brings home a salary at the end of the month, then nothing like it.

DO note that 'Girl only consideration' means we don't care about family, dowry or values. We just have to like the girl that's all. This is rare.

DON'T be shocked that in this nation of a billion dark people, almost no ads want dark-skinned brides. This is a nation obsessed with fair skin.

DO observe that the matrimonial classifieds in India have replaced the intermediary aunt or the family priest who traditionally brought news of a suitable match in the vicinity. As Indian society gets more cosmopolitan, the more the dependence on marriage bureaus and matrimonial ads for the arranged marriage seekers.

DON'T expect hi-tech in this most ancient of rituals. The internet plays almost no role in arranging marriages within India. It's mainly used by Indians living abroad: the NRI men and women who are looking for 'wives with Indian values'. Indians looking for NRI grooms and brides tend to visit these sites. Horoscopes and photographs are emailed to each other. But by and large, Indians still tap into the newspapers and marriage bureaus.

DON'T be saddened, but in many cases blind obedience

rather than blind love is the rule. Especially in rural India, the arranged marriage is still very restrictive where the boy and the girl don't get to even see each other before the happy day. It's the elders in the family that decide the match. All the two main players have to do is turn up, sit on the *mandap* (the marriage platform) and hope for the best!

But **DON'T** fret. The whole process of choosing a partner is changing in urban India.

There is something called semi-arranged marriages. This is what it means. The parents still run around getting horoscopes matched, putting the word out, sift through photographs and letters received from matrimonial ads. However the girl and the boy have the final veto power. It also means that they arrange to fall in love by meeting a few times before marriage. Young couples prefer to call it "arranged cum love marriage".

'SEEING THE GIRL' is an elaborate process. It varies according to your location. If you are in a village, 'seeing the girl' means seeing her photograph (and if you are the girl, seeing his photograph). In small towns it means the girl is dressed up in a special silk sari for the boy and his family to come to inspect. The girl's achievements and creative talents are flaunted. She has to exhibit

her coyness, speak little and keep her eyes lowered demurely. It's an audition and if she passes the screen test, she gets to play the lead role for the rest of her life!

DO remember that this process is a critical one because the girl's home, her cooking skills, her looks are all under test. The boy's family, auntyji, uncleji and the boy's best friend, descend on the girl's house. The girl walks in carrying a tray with tea and snacks. The test is to exhibit a demure walk, not look straight at the boy and yet balance the tray. When the boy and his mother sip the tea and nod, their approval is not just for the tea.

DO note that the horoscope-matching ritual is the clincher in many an arranged marriage. In the south, it takes place before the girl and the boy meet; and in some parts of the north, it takes place after they have met and approve of each other. Computers also match horoscopes and predict the durability of the match.

DON'T be outraged if you find the universal demand is that the bride be like a cow. It does not mean fat like a cow. It means demure and calm like a cow. This is 'good' because it means she will not be assertive and opinionated.

DO know that traditional families choose 'auspicious date and time' for this ritual. In the north, there is even an auspicious wedding season when all the weddings are held - December to February.

DON'T be shocked when young women tell you that in India you marry not only the man, but also his family. She also has to deal with the boy's parents, sisters and the old and infirm grandmother.

In the grand arranged marriage bazaar of India, marriage bureaus bring in the personal touch that the matrimonial ads lack. They check out all the claims and details of the families of the girl and boy personally. They are like consultants. They keep a stock of photographs, bio-data, and horoscopes.

DON'T be shocked to hear of detective agencies doing snooping and some pre-matrimonial investigations for families seeking matches. They'll be checking on backgrounds, whether there are any black sheep in the family or skeletons in the closet, lifestyle, claims about salaries and values, and so on.

Suitable boy

Boys are not on display like the girl is, but there are some universal qualities of 'the most suitable boy'.

DO look for 'NRI' or 'H1B' in matrimonial ads. NRI means the Indian living abroad (Non Resident Indian); H1B visa means the Silicon Valley Indian techie living in paradise awaits your daughter abroad. It works both ways. Many NRIs come back to look for the typical, traditional Indian bride to infuse a bit of Indian culture into their lives abroad. The internet comes in handy here. Some break the ice through a net-chat before buying a ticket to come back to India to see the girl.

DO expect trouble if you fall in love with an Indian and want to marry. Eyebrows will be raised and you will become the subject of a family scandal. Don't take it personally if the auntyji swoons at the news. It's not you, it's her stereotype image of a morally depraved foreigner. You just do not share her cultural values.

Eventually they will come around. You just have to convince them you are not a drug-taking hippie.

The wedding ceremony

The marriage ritual has many variations but there are basically two ways of playing this: in the South, it's a simplistic, religious affair while in the north it's an excuse to have a week long party. It's a flamboyant, boisterous - almost in your face - display of wealth. Even the most austere of ceremonies include at least two functions each from the girl and boy's side. If you are invited, do go and take in all the colour, family drama, good (very rich) food and ostentation. And do pop an indigestion pill before you sleep because the rich food rather than the alcohol will give you a grim morning after. Unfortunately there is no medicine to help you digest this ostentatious display of wealth!

DON'T underestimate the pomp and show. This is not a function. It's a pantomime. At the very least, there is the wedding ceremony hosted by the bride, followed by a reception a day later, given by the groom. These are usually accompanied by a *sangeet* (song and dance evening), which precedes the wedding. Expect loud boisterous music, raunchy songs, and lots of dancing, especially by the old and infirm. Don't be too surprised to find the old and infirm auntyji suddenly tucks in the loose end of her sari around her waist and does a number that'll have you blushing.

DO look out for the eunuchs. Especially in the North, the garishly dressed *hijras* (eunuchs) will land up at your doorstep at the day of the wedding. They'll clap their hands in a rather distinctive manner and ask for money. If you give them, they'll sing and dance and bless the couple. If you don't they'll make your life miserable by taunting the guests - some even strip off their clothes and cause a social embarrassment. Moreover, their blessings are considered auspicious, so it's best to go in for the pay-off, rather than a confrontation.

DO dance, even if you are a bashful man. Tradition is that only women are allowed to attend the *sangeet*. But this is one party where men are allowed to gate crash. This is also the one time where promiscuity is the norm, and there is an open license to flirt. It's also an opportunity to 'fix' other matches and introduce eligible partners, since both sides are on their best display. So if you fancy an Indian spouse, now's the time to try out your charms.

DO get your hands coloured with *mehendi* (henna). This is a ritual for the bride, and it takes place on the morning of the wedding where the bride and her girl friends cover their hands and feet with henna - an Indian herb which stains orange patterns. A traditional game is to write the groom's name in between the intricate design on the bride's hand. He has to then search for his name. In the old days when the bride and groom rarely met each other before they got married, this was one way of breaking the ice! Yes, it's so much simpler to go out for a cup of coffee. But then why simplify a complicated thing and take all the fun out of it?

DON'T try figuring that one out: you're not an Indian so you'll never understand. In cities, however, even arranged marriages allow a degree of intimacy before they are finalised. But the game has become a part of the wedding ritual. Do realize that in India, the *raison d'etre* for most actions is not logic, but tradition.

DON'T be startled if the groom is roaming around barefoot. He hasn't forgotten his shoes, they've been stolen. The bride's friends steal the groom's shoes and he has to pay a mutually agreed price to get them back. The bargaining is for real - these little women all grow up to be efficient housewives who'll haggle their way through the monthly grocery shopping.

DO watch out for the wedding band. The groom arrives at the wedding on horseback flanked by a singing and dancing, semi-drunk crowd of friends and relatives. He is accompanied by a marching band playing the latest Hindi film songs. Sometimes he may even arrive on an elephant but he always departs in a car.

DON'T keep looking at your watch. Like the rest of India, the groom is never on time. This is not the fault of the poor elephant. It is part of the ritual to keep the bride and her family waiting. And guessing. In some smaller towns and villages, the lower the dowry, the more the groom's family delay their arrival to show their displeasure. Nothing subtle about the nuances here.

DON'T think its over just yet. The bridal pair then goes to the *mandap* (raised platform with a fire and priest and close relatives of the bride and groom). The *pundit* (Hindu priest) recites the scripture (seldom understood by anyone) and the bride and groom proceed to walk around the fire seven times. Each circle represents food, strength, wealth, happiness, children, cattle and devotion. This ceremony could take up to three hours but most people ' arrange' it with the *pundit* to make it shorter. The bride is also expected to touch her betrothed's feet. He is now officially her protector and she is acknowledging that she has exchanged her father for another dominating, male figure in her life. But if the woman is financially independent, she dispenses with the feet-touching ritual. Garlands are also exchanged between the two. They are now officially married. Now you can go home and rest your aching feet.

DON'T be alarmed to see a grown man cry during *kanyadaan*. This literally means 'donating the virgin girl' and is perhaps the most emotional moment in the entire wedding drama. Her father gives his daughter away to the groom. Of course, in big cities, the girl in question may not necessarily be a virgin. But that doesn't take away from the filial emotion of the moment.

DO note, this is what is loosely known as a Punjabi wedding. Most Indian weddings follow this pattern, while weaving in different rituals followed by different castes.

A Sikh wedding

DON'T crib if you're not a morning person, but a Sikh wedding is a morning event. Only instead of going around the fire the bridal pair go around the Holy Book and the ceremony is shorter, simpler and more sober. No horses, no elephants during the wedding. Don't feel cheated; these make an appearance at the reception afterwards.

A Tamil wedding

DON'T break into a song and dance, as this is a very traditional affair. The wedding ceremony usually takes place in the morning, followed by lunch. A typical Tamil wedding would serve you food on a plantain (banana) leaf. And don't ask for a spoon or napkins. They would think you are being difficult. It's a two-day affair but the groom does not arrive on a horse. There is almost no dancing but there is singing. There is also a ceremony called *Nelangu* where the bride and groom play 'games', with hundreds of auntyjis and unclejis watching and making assessments about which the dominant partner would be.

DO ask the oldest lady there, and if she has her hearing aid on and can figure out your accent, she'll tell you that it is a legacy of the child-marriage days, where the games kept the young couple entertained in between long rituals. Now, it helps to keep the guests entertained in between those long rituals! Instead of the seven rounds of fire, there are three. And the bride sits on her father's lap as he gives her away.

A Muslim wedding

DON'T complain if you've seen it all before during your visit to Dubai. The wedding ceremony or *nikaah* is conducted by a *mullah* (Muslim priest) and follows the same pattern as in Islamic countries. Unlike other wedding ceremonies, the bride and groom sit in separate rooms while they are married. The *mullah* first goes to the bride and asks her if she accepts the groom. She is asked this question thrice and has to say yes all three time for the marriage to be valid. After which the *mullah* goes to the groom and asks him the same question, three times. For the Muslim wedding, twice is simply not enough.

DO stay for dinner. The wedding is followed by a *waleema*, a dinner hosted by the boy's side, the next evening. The *waleema* celebrates the consummation of the marriage. In fact, in the old days, the stained bed-sheet would be on display at the dinner. You're shocked? This is one practice that has been done away with!

Christian weddings

DO get to the church on time. Indianised Christian weddings take place in the church as in the West. This is one ceremony where the bride can wear white at a wedding in India. However instead of a white dress, she usually wears a sari. The bit about kissing the bride is not part of the ceremony, but is often included on request.

Some general rules

DON'T expect alcohol.

Apart from the expense - as one is expected to serve the best at weddings - it is not in keeping with the religious nature of the occasion. Moreover, the immediate family needs to stay sober for the religious rituals. But don't worry, there will always be an illicit bootlegger on the premises who'll spike your innocuous looking soft drink.

Just ask for the youngest male relative! Alcohol could however be served during the *sangeet* and reception (a dinner the day after the wedding).

DON'T kiss the bride.

Unless you are the bridegroom. And that too never on the lips. At least

not in public. A handshake or a *namaskar* will suffice for both.

DO bring a gift.

Any household item will do. You can also put cash in an envelope and hand it either to the couple, or the parents of the side that invited you. Usually the cash gifts go to the parents to help them pay for the reception. Do not, however, gift perishable items as in most cases the gifts are unwrapped after the honeymoon.

DON'T wear black or white, if you're a woman.

Both are funereal colours and considered inauspicious for women. Men however, wear a black formal suit. They may also wear white but at the very grave aesthetic risk of being compared to Jitendra, a B-Class Hindi movie actor known for his penchant for a white suit and white leather shoes! Indian weddings bring out the brightest and gaudiest colours so don't waste the sartorial licence. It's probably your only chance to wear the loudest colours - and yet be considered well dressed.

DO wear your silks, especially at the South Indian weddings. Don't be fooled by the lack of ostentation. And do wear lots of gold so that you resemble a Christmas tree covered in baubles. Wear jasmine flowers in your hair. But in the north, stick to a girl's best friend - diamonds - since flowers will be mistaken for poverty.

DON'T be confused by the coloured turbans.

As if there wasn't enough colour on the women, the men will be wearing gaily coloured headgear to add to sense of occasion and fun. It also has a practical purpose. The colours distinguish the girl's side from the boy's. So while one side will wear red the other will be in pink.

DO keep track of the coloured headgear as this will help you keep an eye on the dynamics of the 'boy's side' and the 'girl's side'. The boy's set of coloured turbans will demand to be pampered while the other side will run around to fulfil their whims.

DON'T be scandalised by the dowry.
It's a social stigma and a criminal offence, but even the rich and cultured ask for dowry. If they are too sophisticated, they will not openly demand it. But make no mistake. They expect it. The demands vary from household items like a television and fridge to a share in the father-in-law's business. The wife's harmonious stay in her in-law's home depends a great deal on her dowry.

DO read the small items in the newspapers. The euphemism for dowry deaths is 'kitchen accidents'. Don't be fooled. The social malpractice of burning the bride for not bringing enough dowry is still prevalent. A book that deals with this problem goes by the telling title: *Brides are not for Burning*. Recent statistics show that there were as many as 2,000 dowry deaths in the north Indian state of Uttar Pradesh in the year 2001.

Attending funerals

DO wear black or white. Widows wear white. Mourners dress in black or white. However, soft pastel colours are also acceptable. But do avoid the cheerful pinks and the jaunty reds.

DON'T attend the cremation if you are a woman. In India, women are not supposed to go to the cremation or burial grounds, but an exception is made for the immediate family. It is a male, preferably the eldest son, who performs the last rites. Hindus cremate their dead. Muslims bury them. After a cremation, the ashes are immersed in the holy river Ganges. Again this is a ritual for the nearest male relative who usually shaves his hair and wears white as a mark of respect.

DO save some of your tears. The worst is yet to come. Sometimes the widow is also required to shave her head. And in the more orthodox families, the widow will continue wearing white even after the mourning period is over. And just to drive the message home, she is also banned from wearing a *bindi* (the coloured dot on the forehead) and *sindoor* (a red powder in the parting of her hair that indicates a married woman). As a melodramatic gesture, (remember, the Indians love their drama, even if the occasion is a sombre one), the freshly bereaved widow will wipe off her *sindoor* and break her glass bangles. In traditional families, she will also be considered 'impure' and will not be allowed to remarry.

DO shed a tear now because the men have no such restrictions! No surprises here. India is after all a male dominated society and how else can a man assert his self worth if he is so easily replaced? If, however, a widow remarries, the couple will be ostracized by the village. Or at best, remarriage will be seen as a favour bestowed on the widow and she will have to spend the rest of her life telling her husband how grateful she is. Happily, this attitude does not prevail in the cities where a widow can wear colour, bangles and bindi, once the mourning period is over. And, Praise the Lord, she can even remarry without being treated as a charity case.

DON'T expect cooked food. Rites and rituals play an important role in Indian life. So, it is with death. No food is cooked in the house of death until the mourning is over. This can go on for four days (*chautha*) or thirteen days (*tervi*). However, in the metropolitan cities, where life is fast-paced, even death has its loopholes. The rules hold good until the body has been cremated or buried and one night has passed.

DO not bring gifts. Despite the Hindu belief in an afterlife, funerals are not a happy occasion and there is no pretext to cloak them as such. There is no wake, although food and refreshments are available at the prayer ceremony.

DON'T ask for wine. No alcohol of any kind will be offered. Out of respect, you could offer flowers to the dead. Before cremation, this could be at the feet of the body. Afterwards, there is always a garlanded photograph on display. But strictly no gifts, not even cash.

FESTIVALS

India

Diwali: Bright lights: Prayer on the lips and money on the mind

Known as the festival of lights, ironically the celebration takes place on the darkest night in autumn, also known as the night of the new moon. It's a festival of lights and firecrackers. A celebration of the triumph of good over evil. And a time for *Lakshmi Puja* - prayer to the Goddess of Wealth and Prosperity. This is probably the only time when it's okay to worship wealth!

DO wear new clothes. Since *Diwali* also ushers in the Hindu new year, it's off with the old and on with the new.

DON'T look a gift horse in the mouth. During the day itself sweets and gifts are exchanged with friends and relatives. However, over time, this ritual involves more one-upmanship and less goodwill. Some use this opportunity as a form of legalized bribes and send expensive gifts to woo influential big-wigs. The old school sent out dried fruits on a silver platter. Now, gifts of a more exotic nature do the rounds: electronic gadgets, gold and silver idols of Lakshmi, crystal, china...

DO pray for money and don't feel venal about doing so. It's okay.

The *Diwali* evening takes on a sombre note. It's time to pray and hope that all the gifts have their desired effect! After which lights and candles are lit. According to the epic *Ramayana*, Lord Ram and his wife Sita reached Ayodhya (in Uttar Pradesh) on this day after 14 years of exile. To welcome them, the streets were illuminated. The light is also supposed to guide the Goddess Lakshmi into your home. So regardless of electricity bills, leave your hotel lights on throughout the night!

DON'T be prissy. Do gamble. But that's not all. Cards and gambling form a crucial part of the *Diwali* fever. And folklore has it that whoever loses on *Diwali* night, wins the rest of the year.

DON'T expect lavish gifts in the South. As expected, the South has a more cautious approach to the festivities. They burn their crackers in the morning rather than making an evening event out of it. And instead of wishing each other Happy *Diwali*, they solicitously ask each other *"Ganga snaan kiya"*? (Have you had a dip in the holy river?) No, you're not supposed to go looking for the Ganges in the south. It's a way of asking: have you had a bath? That's it. No cards, no ostentatious exchange of presents. It's the south, remember.

Durga Puja: woman power, at least in religious imagination

Durga Puja or *Kali Puja* is popularly celebrated in the eastern part of India and in some states in the south. Practically all of West Bengal goes on a holiday binge for five days. Durga or Kali is one of the most venerated and feared goddesses in the Hindu pantheon. She is looked upon as a symbol of power and strength who killed the evil demon king Mahishasur.

DON'T go by stereotypes. As you can see, the myth of the cow-like, meek, submissive Indian woman just fell through. She can also be a destructive force, so be careful how you tangle with her.

DON'T be surprised. It's yet another triumph of good over evil. It is said that every year Durga descends to earth, along with her four children for nine days. These precede *Diwali* and are known as the *Navaratas*, a time that is marked by Indians in fasting and abstaining from liquor and meat. On the tenth day, Durga returns to her consort, Lord Shiva, and this is celebrated as *Dashera*, the day Rama defeated Ravana the evil King of Lanka. (Triumph of good versus evil is a recurring theme in Indian legendary life). It is said that even the Hindu God Ram worshipped Durga for nine days before he killed Ravana on the tenth.

DO burn an effigy. Huge effigies of the evil King Ravana and his two brothers are burnt all over the country in celebration of *Dashera*. Do go and take in the atmosphere of a village fair, with balloons, Indian delicacies and street plays all thrown in.

Raksha Bandhan: if only a thread could protect you

This is a festival dear to the hearts of Indian women. It takes place on a full moon day in July/August. The ceremony involves praying for the well being and long life of brothers and ends with the tying of a string of red thread around the brothers' wrists.

Raksha means protection and *bandhan* means to tie. Sister is asking her brother to protect her. As a token of his good intentions, he bestows a gift, usually money, to her. So for the sister, the *rakhi* is also an investment bond, where she is guaranteed an annual return!

DO get yourself a *rakhi* brother or a sister. In modern times, *rakhis* have spawned a whole new cottage industry of relationships. A *rakhi* brother need not be a blood relative or a boy friend. Something in between more like it.

The festival of Karva Chauth: if I starve, you will live longer

Once every autumn, on the fourth day after the full moon, Hindu married women in the north starve themselves so their 'beloved' husbands can enjoy a long life.

In some mystical way, the day of starvation also ensures that they'll be married to the same man during their next seven lives. This is supposed to be their declaration of love for their present husbands. The wife takes no food, no water and no tea from dawn until the moon appears at night. It does not matter even if the husband is a no good wife beater. Tradition still dictates that she starves for his long life.

DO look for the central protagonist in the ritual, the moon. Only when it appears in the sky, can millions of wives end their suffering. The moon represents the husband: as the moon shines forever, so shall husbands live forever... In the evening, on every rooftop and every balcony, women dressed in their finest silk saris and gold jewellery crane their necks to catch a glimpse of the elusive moon.

DO be patient, because invariably, the moon on that night is late, adding to the tension and anxiety. Some women faint. Well fed husbands who have heard their wives whine all day in hunger, pace up and down.

DO remember: it's not about the moon or the food. It's about the husband. When the moon eventually appears, hungry wives rush to say a word or two of prayer offering flowers and rice grains to boot. Then they view the moon through a kitchen sieve and look at their moon-faced husbands through the sieve. After which they bend down to touch the men's feet. Now they can eat.

DON'T miss the social comment. This ritual is so that the wife does not outlive her husband. At the root of the festival is the status of the Indian widow. Although things are getting better, a woman's life changes forever when she becomes a widow. As we've described, she can no longer wear the jewellery and the decorative *bindi* on her forehead, vermilion in her hair and the bright-coloured saris of a married woman. She is not even supposed to attempt to look good. Worse can happen. But the festival of *Karva Chauth* remains. Does it work? Apparently not. Statistics show that the Indian woman outlives the Indian man. No matter, statistics fall short when pitted against Indian beliefs.

DO look for the 90s twist. This festival has seen a strange revival among the urban, English-speaking, cell phone-toting middle class. The Indian movies and the advertising world have transformed this ancient ritual into a modern day Indian equivalent of Valentine's Day. "How much do you really love your wife as she starves for you," seems to be the message for husbands. Enough to buy her a gift? A new sari? A diamond ring? A gold necklace? A DVD player? And that microwave oven that will make her life easier?

DON'T be surprised if you glimpse tradition wrapped in a mini skirt. These days *karva chauth* is also promoted as one of the true Indian traditions where a woman gets to prove how Indian she really is. She could be wearing mini-skirts and tight pants all year long, but if she fasts for her husband on this day, she is a true Indian at heart.

Holi: Rite of spring

This is supposed to be a festival of colours to welcome the onset of spring after a long winter and following the wheat harvest. It comes in the month of *Phagun* in February or March. It is not 'played' in the south. In a joyful celebration Indians throw water balloons and coloured powder at each other.

The night before *holi*, neighbours gather to light bonfires called *holikas* at crossroads. Children roast green gram and potatoes in the flames. Bonfires date back to the days of King Hiranyakashyap, when he ordered his son Prahlad, a devotee of the Hindu God Vishnu, to be burnt alive. Hiranyakashyap asked his sister Holika to wear magic clothes that would not catch fire and hold Prahlad tightly on her lap so that he would die in the flames and she would not be hurt. Holika could not bear to kill the little boy. So she quietly transferred the magic clothes to Prahlad, sacrificing herself but saving the little boy. Holika went to heaven for her pious act. That's the story of its origin. Now here's what holi is really all about!

Coloured water is squirted at others from a *pichkari*, handheld water pumps and water guns. Children fill balloons with water, sometimes filled with coloured paint, and throw them at passers by, including you, our dear visitor. Some just prefer to throw a bucket full of water from their rooftops at any passing target. But the 'cultured and the dignified' stay away from the water and instead smear neon coloured *gulal* (coloured powder) on people's faces.

DO join in the water celebrations if you are courageous. But make sure you are not alone, go with a group of friends whom you trust.

DO be brave enough to wear white. By the end of the day your nice white shirt will be a patchwork of all the colours that have been thrown on you.

DO try your best to protect your eyes from the *gulal*. Old people will bless you by smearing bright colours all over your face and hair. By and large people still use harmful, toxic chemical dyes. You might consider wearing dark glasses.

DO remember that Hindu mythology is full of references to flirtatious games played by Lord Krishna, who uses the excuse of *holi* to sing and dance with young maidens. Krishna is said to have played *holi* with so much gusto that even today the songs sung during the festival relate the pranks that he played with his sweethearts.

DON'T think it's just about the fun-filled mirth of swoosh and splash. It is also a day when fathers keep their daughters locked in the house as 'nice girls' don't venture out onto the streets. For women this rite of spring could turn into water terror at the hands of marauding gangs of youths waiting to ambush (and worse) hapless maidens. So girls, don't venture out alone.

DON'T accept drinks or milk or sweets from strangers, especially if they are green (the sweets, not the people). The biggest kick of *holi* is the marijuana-doctored drinks, called *bhang*, flowing as freely as the coloured water. The day's revelry can end with a *bhang* with you too intoxicated to move.

Id

Muslims celebrate *Id* with all its tradition and rituals. This marks the cessation of Ramadan, the month of fasting, which ends with the sighting of the new moon. Although Hindus do not keep the fast, they are often invited to the party to help their Muslim neighbours break it. Delicious kebabs (meat cutlets) and sweet *seyaiyyan* (a kind of vermicelli) is served, and there is much hugging and cries of *"Id mubarak"* (Happy *Id*).

DON'T get confused with another *Id* called *Bakra-Id*, where a goat is sacrificed. (*Bakra* means goat but for the poor goat the celebrations are not at all happy). The goat sacrifice resembles Abraham's sacrifice of his son to show his obedience to the Lord's command. The goat is fed and fattened before it is beheaded.

Christmas

The festival lost its official air after the British Raj but it's still celebrated with pomp, greeting cards, presents and even carols. It's like a *diwali* in winter, and is celebrated by christians and non-christians. In the biggest cities, five star hotels and clubs will host christmas eve parties.

DO realise that Indians are more familiar with the notion of a red suited santa claus than with Jesus Christ and the biblical connotations of the festival. For most, it's a time to meet friends, sing Jingle Bells and drink wine.

DON'T worry, christians do go to church for midnight mass. But for most Indians it's a precursor to the New Year celebrations, christmas tree and all. While you'll get the plum cake and the wine, don't look for the turkey at the christmas spread. Also don't expect the mistletoe hanging from the roof - this is India, remember.

Republic day

DON'T be startled if India's Republic Day parade (January 26) makes you wonder for a moment if you are in China, North Korea or Russia! Critics decry it as nothing more than a leftover from the Stalinist era! But it's much more than that.

DO take in the event. Usually a grandiose display of military muscle, the Republic Day parade marks the anniversary of the adoption of India's constitution. The country's top leaders, officials and foreign dignitaries are present. Tanks, guns and missiles are displayed with pride while soldiers march towards the Presidential palace. Air Force jets circle the skies and sprinkle rose petals. The entire event is telecast live on national TV and the ritual is watched by millions in patriotic fervour.

DO note that New Delhi traffic comes to a halt until noon for the parade. Elaborate rehearsals begin at least a week before the day itself.

INDIAN
SUPERSTITION

If you read this book make sure it's on a Tuesday. If you buy this book in India, pay the money with your right hand. If your money cascades to the floor and you step on it by mistake, please pick it up and bring it to your forehead before using it.

There is list of Dos and Don'ts for Indians based on millions of superstitions - longer than those that we have given in this book. The only problem is Indians do not always know how to separate religion from superstition. Here's a sample for you.

DON'T step out of your house in a group of three and don't go for important business in a group of three. The work will not get done, they say. If you have no choice, one of you could step out first and walk a few yards, then the other two could follow.

DO stop if a black cat crosses your path. It's a bad omen. Wait a minute, until somebody else walks ahead of you. Then you are okay.

DON'T call out to somebody as they leave the house or office. It brings bad luck for that person. If you do, they will come back in, sit for a few minutes and then try leaving again. Keep your tongue locked this time around.

DON'T sneeze as somebody leaves the house as the same ritual applies.

DO expect guests if a crow caws in front of your house in the morning. In some parts of India people believe that when a crow cackles you can be sure somebody is lying. Doesn't seem to work on Indian politicians though.

DON'T sweep the house after sunset, as it brings bad luck. The Hindu Goddess of Wealth, Lakshmi, leaves the house as night falls. It's a bad omen to cut your nails after sunset too.

DON'T place your handbag on the floor. The money in it will be spent too soon.

DON'T walk under a ladder, it brings bad luck.

DO take care not to keep your hand on the floor when you eat. In the south of India it is feared that the nutrition from the food flows out of your body.

DO take a shower immediately after returning from a funeral. Otherwise you will bring death home with you.

DO squash a lime under the front wheels of your new car before you use it. It keeps accidents away. In India, the chances of accidents are so high, this 'insurance' is a small price to pay.

DO let the eunuch bless your newborn child. Both a eunuch's blessing and curse comes true. Eunuchs take advantage of this and arrive in a flock when they hear of a marriage or birth. They demand money for their blessings and threaten a curse if not paid. People pay out of fear.

DO get ready for good fortune if the left eye of a woman flutters involuntarily.

DON'T wear black to Hindu functions and festivals. It doesn't matter if you believe black is in or makes you look thin. It is an inauspicious colour. And never, never wear black to a wedding. You'll be frowned upon.

DO take care of your bangles at a Hindu wedding. If they break it is a bad omen. In Hindu culture bangles are broken only when a woman becomes a widow.

DO listen for the screech of the gekko, a small house lizard that scuttles across walls and ceilings. If it screeches from the east, whatever you are thinking at that moment will come true. If it screeches from the west, whatever you are thinking will fail. This is because ancestors take the form of the gekko and return to earth to warn about the future.

EVEN I'M CONFUSED

DON'T let the dog bark and howl at night. If you hear it, it brings news of death.

DO check the *rahu kala* if you are in the south of India. All the Hindu calendars in the south have a one-and-a-half hour period every day which is meant to be inauspicious. Almost all politicians check the timings.

DON'T go out or eat during eclipses. It is a bad omen. A pregnant woman should not go out during the eclipse as her child could be deformed. Indians believe that harmful rays during an eclipse penetrate the earth and may cause harm.

DON'T take or give things with your left hand. Left is inauspicious for Indians. When you enter a house or an office for the first time, enter with the right foot first.

INDIAN TRIVIA

India

India cannot be neatly compartmentalized into an established set of manners and mannerisms. There is a whole theatre that is being enacted on the sidelines - and there is no script that one can use as a reference point. However, this chapter offers some guidelines to help you deal with a few of the idiosyncrasies, much of the trivia and a bit of the flavour that is the essence of India.

DON'T be shocked to see the most private acts in public. There aren't too many public toilets in India. But no one misses them either as any empty public space is used as a toilet.

DON'T attempt a long conversation with a man who is walking purposefully with a mug toward a field. He is a man in a hurry.

DON'T look out of the windows of your railway carriage at dawn; railway lines are prime toilet space for the nearby residents.

DO look out for the Singhs. It's never the first name. Generally a middle name or a surname. All Singhs are not Sikhs, but all Sikhs are Singhs. In orthodox families, female Sikhs are however, not Singhs, their middle name is generally Kaur. Note too that the wife of a Mr. Singh, if he is a Sikh is Mrs. Kaur. But don't worry. You can address your dinner invitations to Mr. and Mrs. Singh.

DON'T be startled if Happy and Pinky and Bubbles and Snoopy are actually huge, burly, turbaned Sikhs. Indians love their nicknames.

DO take an interest in the initials in people's names when you are in the South. The initials not only stand for their father's name, but also the name of their ancestral village. For example, when you meet a T. V. Raman, the "T" stands for the village or the district, and the "V" for the father's name. But you can call him Raman.

DON'T ever hit a cow, ditto for holy men. Always remember, for a Hindu the cow is akin to a mother figure and often treated better. If you see a cow standing in the middle of the road blocking traffic, don't try to do anything about it. It's a familiar sight, even in the most urban of areas. Never argue with a cow. The cow is always right.

DON'T be rude to the man dressed in saffron even though he looks like a fraud. He may even try to tell your future. If he is talking to you, he is generally interested only in your money. Be polite and ignore him. Being rude can be taken as a religious affront. Don't however, be surprised if he speaks English - some cater exclusively to foreigners. Just remember, an honest-to-goodness holy man will be more interested in your spiritual wealth than your foreign exchange!

DON'T join street processions. The Mahatma taught Indians how to protest, and they're still protesting. When they are revolting, people will stop traffic at the city's busiest junction. Shops will be closed on a working day to protest against something or other. It's a national pastime.

DON'T accept torn Indian currency. You can't pass it off next time you buy something. Indians react with a great deal of hostility when you pay with torn or old notes. It is easier to pass off counterfeits.

DO be careful when you cross the road. **DON'T** expect civil behaviour from the traffic. The concept of a pedestrian zebra crossing doesn't work here except as a mere design on the tarmac. The cars will not stop for you to cross first. And there is nothing you can do about it. If you apply the rules of Europe you'll be dead.

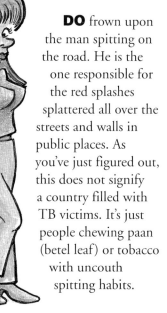

DO frown upon the man spitting on the road. He is the one responsible for the red splashes splattered all over the streets and walls in public places. As you've just figured out, this does not signify a country filled with TB victims. It's just people chewing paan (betel leaf) or tobacco with uncouth spitting habits.

DON'T expect the Indian cowboy to be a Marlboro Man. In rural India they smoke the *beedi* rather than a cigarette as it is known in the western world. This is a local cigarette made with tobacco leaves. It's much cheaper than the branded variety and surprisingly very popular in America and Europe. Indian students exchange *beedis* for other favours in the west. So buy a couple of packets to take back home for the 'connoisseurs'.

DON'T be surprised but India has washing-men rather than washing machines. These are India's answer to the Laundromats. The local *dhobi* collects and delivers clothes to your doorstep. He takes two days to wash and iron them since he beats your delicate fabrics against a stone, perhaps by the river, and then hangs them out to dry before ironing them. Expect a little wear and tear. If you are interested, he will also provide you with local gossip. A little tip will do wonders for his efficiency.

DO drink from a *kulhar*. These are the drink and smash earthen cups, better know as the Indian alternative to plastic cups and much more hygienic. Beats dirty glasses any day. Roadside stalls and railway stations serve very sweet tea in them.

DON'T miss the Red Dot. That's the *bindi.* The red dot on a woman's forehead denotes she is a Hindu and is married. However these days, even unmarried girls sport the red dot. From a marital statement, it's become a fashion footnote. But a widow usually avoids it. Some children may also have a black mark on their face. But don't write that off as a dirty face. The idea is to smudge the child's beauty just enough to keep the evil eye away.

DON'T miss out on a visit to the *vaid.* A *vaid* is an ayurveda practitioner. This is an ancient system of Indian medicine, now very much in vogue with the Western world. The practitioner feels your pulse and tells you what is wrong with you. He makes his own medicines from natural herbs and sometimes even pearls, gold and silver. **DON'T** scoff at this. If you've got yourself a genuine *vaid*, it does work. In villages, he is often the only medical man.

DO get your hand read. But don't believe all that you hear. The palmist reads your palm, makes predictions of your future and tells you about your past. The predictions range from the serious: "you will get problems in your marriage until next June" to the trivial: "you will buy a new car". If you go to an astrologer, he will ask you your date, time and place of birth and proceed to make a chart. He will also make predictions and probably tell you which stone to wear to avert the evil influence of *Shani* (the effect of the planet Saturn on your astrological chart). In fact, any phase of bad luck is always attributed to the *Shani* and many remedies are suggested to overcome this. One of these is to donate coins (not paper money) on a Saturday.

DO have fun with the fortune telling cows and parrots. It's not always a man who tells your fortune. You will be introduced to cows that claim to read your fortune by a nod or a shake of a head. And even a parrot that, upon being released from the cage, picks out a card that predicts your future. One thing is for sure, no one will predict a Tall Dark Stranger in your life. Indians are very colour conscious (more about that elsewhere.)

DON'T make eye contact. You meet touts everywhere - from Five Star hotels to street corners. They will offer to procure whatever you are seeking. And offer you 'bargain rates'. Needless to say, Be Wary. Beggars can be found on most streets, and all traffic lights. It's a thriving industry. Avoid them. Walk past without eye-contact. They look upon foreigners as easy prey. Engage in conversation or give money to one and you will be surrounded in no time. If you are moved by their plight, do offer food rather than money. One good point - Beggars don't mug you and they don't abuse foreigners.

DO get your shoes polished: You'll find the shoeshine boy in every crowded locality. He will pester you and follow you around until you are bullied into getting your shoes polished. It doesn't matter if your shoes are made of suede or canvas. He'll still offer to polish them. And do a good job while he's at it. But do beware of the shoeshine-boy mafia who 'accidentally' spit or throw gooey stuff on your shoes to force you to get them cleaned.

DON'T miss the ear cleaner: Despite all talk of poor hygiene, India is probably the only place where you'll find a professional ear cleaner on the streets. Some even carry a government of India

approved tag. The instrument is a homemade version of the Johnson ear bud: some cotton wrapped on a stick. They'll ask for Rs.700. Pay them Rs. 20. You may however decide that it's safer to stick to the regular ear bud.

DO get your head massaged under a tree. These are barbers, not hair stylists. They can be found near most shopping areas, working on the streets in the open, under a tree, with just a chair. Also known locally as The Sun 'n' Shade shops. For a very small fee, they will give you a haircut, a shave, and massage your head with strong smelling oil. But remember they use long razors that look like knives. And are not hygienically cleaned, so if he nicks you by mistake, you may need more than just a band-aid to fix the damage. But the massage is very good.

USEFUL PHRASES

India

These are not grammatical or complete sentences. They are just a colloquial way of speaking. Only Hindi phrases are given. When visiting south India, use English.

Shopping

How much?	*Kitna hai?*
Make it slightly less.	*Thoda kum.*
Too expensive.	*Bahut mehenga hai.*
Show me that please?	*Woh dikhayenge?*
How much a metre?	*Ek metre kitne ka?*
Can you show me some more?	*Aur dikhayenge?*
What time do the shops open?	*Market kab khulega?*
Do you have other colours?	*Isme aur rang hai kya?*
I will buy it if it's cheaper.	*Sastaa doge to lenge.*
Is the colour fast?	*Rang pakka hai kya?*
Do you accept cards?	*Credit card chalega?*

Road, Air and Train Travel

How far?	*Kitna door?*
How much longer?	*Aur kitni door?*
Where is the petrol pump?	*Petrol pump kidhar hai?*
This seat is mine.	*Yeh seat meri hai.*
Is the train on time?	*Train time pe hai?*
What time does the train leave?	*Train kab chalegi?*
How much is the ticket?	*Ek ticket ka kitna?*
Can you help me please?	*Kya meri madad karenge?*
Stop, I want to get off here.	*Rokiye, mujhe yahaan utarna hai.*
Let's go.	*Chalo.*
Is there mineral water?	*Bisleri miltee hai kya?*
What is this?	*Yeh kya hai?*
Where is the bathroom?	*Bathroom kahaan hai?*
How is the road ahead?	*Aage road theek hai?*
HELP!	*Bachao!*
Stop Thief!	*Chor chor! Pakdo pakdo!*
When is the next stop?	*Agla stop kab hai?*
My luggage is stolen!	*Mera samaan chori ho gayi.*
Where is the TC?	*TC kidhar hai?*
Please confirm my ticket.	*Mera ticket confirm karo please.*
The car has broken down.	*Gaadi kharab ho gayee.*
It is very hot.	*Bahut garam hai.*
Can you fix a flat tyre?	*Kya aap tyre badal sakte hain?*

How much per day?	*Ek din ka kitna kiraya?*
How much?	*Kitna?*
May I sit here?	*Yahan baith sakte hain?*
Can you give me a lift?	*Lift milega?*
Is smoking allowed here?	*Yahaan cigarette pee sakte hain kya?*

Weddings

We are from the boy's side.	*Hum ladke wale hain.*
We are from the girl's side.	*Hum ladki wale hain.*
Has the groom arrived?	*Baraat aagayi kya?*
When will the meal be served?	*Khana kab milega?*
The bride is beautiful.	*Ladki bahut sundar hai.*
Congratulations.	*Badhai ho.*

Funerals

Very sorry.	*Bahut afsos hua.*
If there's anything you need please let me know.	*Kisi cheez ki zaroorat ho to mujhe batao.*

Home and hospitality

Hello	*Namaste*
How are you?	*Aap kaise hain?*

My stomach is upset, no dinner please.	*Mera pet kharab hai, mujhe dinner naheen chaahiye.*
I am feeling sleepy.	*Mujhe neend aa rahee hai.*
Can I have tea?	*Kai mujhe chai milega please?*
Where is the toilet?	*Bathroom kidhar hai?*
It's delicious.	*Bahut swaadisht hai.*
I am full.	*Pet bhar gaya.*
Can you wake me up in the morning?	*Kya aap mujhe jaldi jagaa doge?*
No spice.	*Mirchi naheen.*
Thank you.	*Shukriya.*
See you soon.	*Phir milenge.*

Eating out

I want to eat Indian food.	*Desi khana chahiye.*
Is this very spicy?	*Bahut mirchi hai kya?*
What desserts do you have?	*Meetha kya hai?*
Is the food freshly cooked?	*Khana taaza hai kya?*
The tea is cold.	*Chai thandi hai.*
You have overcharged me.	*Tumne zyaada paisa charge kiya hai.*
We will come back again.	*Hum phir aayenge.*
Give me a receipt.	*Bill chahiye.*

Women travellers

Brother	*Bhaisaheb*
Is there any risk?	*Koi khatra to naheen?*
When does it get dark?	*Andhera kab hota hai?*
This man harassed me.	*Yeh aadmi ne mujhe cheda.*
Where can I shop?	*Market kahan hai?*
Where is the chemist?	*Dawai ki dukan kahan hai?*
Leave me alone.	*Mujhe akela chod do.*
I will complain to the police.	*Main police ko report karoongi.*
I am married.	*Main shaadi shudaa hoon.*

Male traveller

Where can I get a drink?	*Sharaab kahan milegi?*
I don't want country liquor.	*Desi naheen chahiye.*
Where can I watch a movie?	*Cinema theatre kidhar hai?*
Are you married?	*Kya aap shaadi shudaa hain?*